# Earning
## Without
## Being
# Employed

# Earning
## — Without —
## Being
# Employed

## 35 Businesses
### Anyone can Start and Run

*Jeff Evarts*

iUniverse, Inc.
Bloomington

Earning Without Being Employed
35 businesses anyone can start and run

Copyright © 2012 Jeff Evarts

iUniverse books may be ordered through booksellers or by contacting:

iUniverse
1663 Liberty Drive
Bloomington, IN 47403
www.iuniverse.com
1-800-Authors (1-800-288-4677)

ISBN: 978-1-4620-6751-0 (sc)
ISBN: 978-1-4620-6752-7 (hc)
ISBN: 978-1-4620-6753-4 (e)

Printed in the United States of America

iUniverse rev. date: 12/20/2011

Earning without being Employed

35 businesses anyone can start and run
*by*
*Jeff Evarts*

*This book is dedicated to my father,*

<u>William Marvin Evarts III</u>

*who taught me about business so thoroughly by his example
that there was almost nothing left to say.*

*I would like to acknowledge the incarnations of Eve that have graced my life:*

Counselor, Redeemer, Lover, Muse, Inspiration,
Twin, Complement and Wellspring

*Thank you all.*

# Contents

**About the Author** . . . . . . . . . . . . . 1

**Mixed Bag** . . . . . . . . . . . . . 3

  1  Sign Language Interpreter . . . . . . . .5

  2  Bicycle Courier . . . . . . . . . . . . .9

  3  Rental Property Manager . . . . . . . 13

  4  Locksmith . . . . . . . . . . . . 17

  5  Taxidermist . . . . . . . . . . . . 21

  6  Well Driller . . . . . . . . . . . . . 25

  7  Traveling Massage Therapist . . . . . . 29

  8  Limousine Driver . . . . . . . . . . . 33

**Municipal Services** . . . . . . . . . . . . 37

  9  Crime Scene Cleanup . . . . . . . . . 41

 10  Tow Truck Operator . . . . . . . . . 45

 11  Snow Plow Operator . . . . . . . . 49

 12  Animal Control Technician . . . . . . 53

**Professional Contracting** . . . . . . . . 57

 13  Plumber . . . . . . . . . . . . . . 63

 14  Carpenter . . . . . . . . . . . . . 65

 15  Electrician . . . . . . . . . . . . . 67

 16  Painter . . . . . . . . . . . . . . 69

 17  Tile & Ceramics Contractor . . . . . . 73

**Foraging** . . . . . . . . . . . . . . 75

   18  Worm Fiddler . . . . . . . . . . . . 77

   19  Gold Panner. . . . . . . . . . . . 83

   20  Marine Logger . . . . . . . . . . 87

   21  Meteor Hunter . . . . . . . . . . . 91

**Animal Services**. . . . . . . . . . . . . . 97

   22  Farrier. . . . . . . . . . . . . . . 99

   23  Large Aquarium Maintenance. . . . 103

   24  Obedience Trainer. . . . . . . . . 107

   25  Traveling Pet Groomer . . . . . . 111

   26  Animal Caretaker . . . . . . . . . 115

**Teaching and Coaching** . . . . . . . . .119

   27  Music Teacher. . . . . . . . . . . 121

   28  Language Teacher . . . . . . . . . 125

   29  Personal Fitness Trainer . . . . . . 129

   30  Dance Instructor . . . . . . . . . 133

**Residential Services** . . . . . . . . . .137

   31  Pool & Spa Maintenance . . . . . 139

   32  Mobile Car Detailing . . . . . . . 143

   33  Exterminator . . . . . . . . . . . 147

   34  Dog Walker . . . . . . . . . . . 151

   35  Handyman . . . . . . . . . . . 155

**Other Business Ideas** . . . . . . . . . .159

**Lessons Learned** . . . . . . . . . . . . .161

    Norm's Story: People's names . . . . . . 161

    Dirk's Story: Make your plan happen . . 162

    Emily's Story: Schedule "other stuff" . . . 163

**Business How-To's** . . . . . . . . . . . .165

    Get and Use a Credit Card Machine . . . 165

    Get Bonded . . . . . . . . . . . . . . 166

    Upgrade Your Vehicle Insurance.. . . . . 166

**Conclusion** . . . . . . . . . . . . . . . .169

**Appendix A: Summary of Jobs** . . . . . .171

**Appendix B: Add-on businesses** . . . . .173

    The Dangers of Mini- or Side- businesses 173

    Notary Public . . . . . . . . . . . . . 173

    Key Duplication . . . . . . . . . . . . 174

    Stuff for Sale . . . . . . . . . . . . . . 174

**Appendix C: Other Resources** . . . . . .175

    Small Business Development Centers . . 175

    Your Chamber of Commerce . . . . . . 175

    The Better Business Bureau (BBB) . . . . 175

    Other local small-business resources . . . 176

Try not to become a man of success, but rather try to become a man of value

—Albert Einstein, 1879 – 1955

# About the Author

Jeff Evarts comes from a family of successful entrepreneurs. At age 6, living in rural New Hampshire, he sold greeting cards door to door to earn money for a chemistry set and his mother operated a for-profit nursery school. In high school and college he consulted, writing software for local businesses, while his father started a manufacturing business that operated throughout Asia. After college and fifteen years of software engineering for companies like Amazon.com and Google, he again left employment and invested in the real estate improvement business his brother-in-law was starting.

Earning income for the owner is the measure of a successful business, and all of these businesses were successful. He brings this experience to the subject matter of this book.

## How this book came about

In May of 2010, a good friend of mine was talking about how hard it was becoming to get an interview in the current job climate. I remarked that *no one* should feel that the application / interview / offer process was the only way to earn money, and suggested he start an independent business instead.

He balked, and challenged me to take my own advice. I agreed, and this book is the result. As a first time author, but long time business owner, I branched out into a whole new field, and I really encourage you to do the same. The book in your hand was written specifically to help you find a way to do it. I hope it serves you well.

—Jeff Evarts

▼

# MIXED BAG

*Jobs you may never have considered.*

The first section is a description of several jobs that are available to almost anyone. (Sign Language Interpreter, Bicycle Courier, Rental Property Manager, Locksmith, Taxidermist, Well Driller, Traveling Massage Therapist, and Limousine Driver) They're examples of jobs that you don't need permission to get: there's no boss, you don't need to open a store, and they're workable by a large variety of people.

# 1
# Sign Language Interpreter
*Speaking for the deaf*

All over the United States there are deaf people who need someone to translate for them. This job is done by professional sign language interpreters. In some cases, the translation is strictly one-way, such as at a conference station which offers the lectures translated into sign. In other cases, such as in court, it will be bidirectional, with you serving as a translator between the deaf and the hearing.

## The Pay

Pay for sign language interpretation varies a lot, depending on the forum in which you are employed. In places where full-time communication with the deaf is a requirement, it may only be a bonus attached to other work done. In places where a sign language interpreter is required for more specific and technical communication, the pay per hour or per service can be larger. Hourly wages between $15 and $40 per hour are normal for people reasonably adept at signing, and rates can exceed $100/hr for people with specialty communication skills, such as specific technical/industry vocabularies. There are even sets of signs for various religions, etc.

## Training

This is the big deal. There are lots of ASL classes available online and probably at your high school, high school extension, and community college. Be warned: not all sign language classes are created equal. You will need the National Interpreter Certification to get any serious job as a sign language interpreter. This certification is available from the Registry of Interpreters for the Deaf. Start by contacting this agency, and ask for their recommended programs in your area.

## Equipment

*Required*
- Comfortable and appropriate clothing.

*Good To Have*
- Notepad & Pencil
- Cellphone with a texting plan

## Licenses Required

You will need to get the National Interpreter Certification.

## Getting Started

*Is this for me?*

While there are some jobs where you're just being videoed signing a soundtrack of other people's voices, for the most part you will be working directly with the deaf. Some may be able to speak, many will not. Often you will be sitting and signing for long periods of time at a stretch. Interpreting for the podium speaker at a conference, for instance. Since sign language is a visual medium, people will be looking at you for sometimes hours at a time. If being in the public eye is a problem for you, Sign Language Interpretation is probably not a good choice.

On the other hand, if you enjoy communicating with people, and assisting those whom other people might pass by; if you would take pride in helping people, enabling them to take part where they otherwise might not, then sign language interpretation may be a great choice for you.

*Market Research*

The market has been thoroughly researched. Demand is high. Every registry I contacted was in need of more interpreters.

### Get Trained

To get trained, first contact RID, and ask them which programs in your area they recommend. As always, shop around, but it's probably best to stay within the recommendations you get from those organizations.

### Get Your Equipment

Happily, there is none. Skip to the next step.

### Do it!

There are national registries where certified sign language interpreters can list their availability. Many states and municipalities also have local registries. Don't forget to contact the emergency services folks, if you're willing to work on their time and place requirements. Fire & Rescue and Police often have need of SLI.

### Get Paid

This varies a lot. There are no fixed rules. In some cases you'll be paid up front, in others after the service is complete, and often (when working with a city or state service) at the end of the month by check. In all cases, you'll have settled the rates before you begin, so you'll know how much to expect when the money eventually arrives.

## Getting Good

There isn't really a consensus among the people I talked to about this. Some stressed technical capabilities to get the jobs others were not qualified to get, some stressed social contact because there's a lot of repeat business out there, still others focused on technique and attention to detail, so that your personal "accent" wasn't in the way of a potentially national audience of watchers. As far as I can tell it's a matter of practice and serving the customer.

## Other Resources

- Registry of Interpreters for the Deaf (RID)
- The National Association for the Deaf (NAD)

Both organizations have online and brick-and-mortar resources available to help you get certified, and can help you get jobs once you are certified.

# 2
# Bicycle Courier

*Have Bike and Backpack, Will Travel*

Bicycle couriers are paid to carry packages from one place to another, typically from one business to another within the same city, town, or borough.

## The Pay

Bicycle couriers are paid based on the expected travel time, typically more per hour for the shorter jobs, to cover for unpaid transit time to the customer and from the destination. Typical pay varies from $15/hr to $40/hr depending on time spent and package care requirements. A half-hour minimum is fairly common.

## Training

No formal training is required, although from a practical perspective, physical fitness is going to be a big factor. Likewise, you are very replaceable for the customer, so appearing professional, trustworthy, and respectful will all contribute greatly to repeat business. Spending some time role-playing with a businessperson friend or even just practicing your dialog in front of a mirror may help.

## Equipment

*Required*

- A bicycle you are very, very comfortable riding
- A sturdy frame backpack for heavy/bulky loads
- A large, soft backpack for carrying lots of little things
- A cellphone that works *everywhere* in your area
- Cologne/Deodorant, comb, towel, etc

If you're delivering to a legal office, hospital, military base, etc., you will want to be able to give yourself a quick cleanup before entering their premises

*Good To Have*

- Sunglasses, Bicycle Helmet, Sunblock
- Tire repair kit, tire pump, water bottle, etc
- Small first aid kit

*Luxuries*

- A cellphone-connectible credit card swiper can be very useful

## Licenses Required

No states currently have statewide licensing for bicycle couriers. Some cities, including Chicago, do. Check with your city hall about that.

Some of your customers may want you to be bonded. Don't worry, this has nothing to do with either handcuffs or a bail bond. Bonding is essentially insurance that you carry which is payable to the customer if you steal or intentionally damage their property. It's usually a matter of registering with a bonding company, and sometimes paying a fee or putting aside some money in an account the bondsman has access to.

## Getting Started

*Is this for me?*

If you don't really enjoy bicycling in all weather, working with different people every day, and spending most of your day by yourself on the road, this job is not for you. If those things appeal to you, this is going to be a lot of fun.

*Market Research*

One way to do this is to join an existing courier company. The wages may be lower, but you don't have to market yourself right off. Another advantage is that it's easier to take a vacation since they have other carriers who can pick up the slack. They may even offer benefits, although that's rare.

Alternatively, if you're running this business by and for yourself, you need to get on the phone and on your bike and hustle around town, dropping off your card and contact information everywhere. Be prepared to have to explain why they should start doing business with you. Most businesses already have some way of getting their packages around town. Whether they're asking Bob in maintenance to do it on his lunch hour, or sending it via FedEx. They already have some way to get this done, and you will need to get them to get them to change the way they do business.

### Get Trained

Hopefully, you can ride a bike. Beyond that, you're on your own.

### Get Your Equipment

As cool as your current bike is, most couriers report that they actually replace their bike, or buy a new one, shortly after starting. This is usually because recreational biking and courier work ask for different things from a bicycle, whether it's toe clips or seat design, carry-ability or brake lever choice, it's usually different than what you're used to. Be prepared to shell out for a new bike as a business expense within your first year.

### Do it!

Every hour you're not on the move with someone's package, you need to be marketing yourself. Pick a start and end time for your service, and when you're not carrying, drive up and down the commercial streets and drop off cards, visit with potential customers, and touch base with your regulars. The more often you do this, the more often your phone rings with a job, and the more money you make.

### Get Paid

Most payments are made up-front, although some customers will insist that the destination will pay. If you're getting paid up-front, you may get cash or a check. If you're getting paid at delivery, it's most likely a check or voucher that you take to someone else in the building. Credit cards can be a problem: If you have a dispatcher, they can take the number over the phone, and verify it from the office. If you're a one-man-band, you're going to need a swiper of some kind, either connected to your cellphone, or the old-style carbon copy kind.

## Getting Good

This has much less to do with good routing and fast pedaling than it does with availability and attitude. While your biking is what gets you paid, your personal interactions are what gets and keeps your customers. Availability is key. You are often being called when something is urgent: the customer needs this widget delivered within the next hour or they lose an account, etc. A busy signal or a vacation day can put a crimp in your relationship that will take time to smooth out. Likewise, taking time to catch your breath, dry off, and comb your hair before you walk into their office separates "the best" from "the rest" in the eyes of both the shipper and the recipient.

## Other Resources

You may want to check out the International Federation of Bicycle Messenger Associations (IFBMA) for worldwide support in this craft.

Beyond that, the courier organizations seem to be local: citywide or smaller. There are far too many to list here. Check with your local bike shops. They will have clubs or at least contacts for you to start with.

# 3
# Rental Property Manager

*Professional problem solver for residential rental properties*

It's fairly common for people who rent out a house they own to live far from that property. If they're professional landlords, they might have properties all over the U.S. Others are families who have moved out of the area but kept the house as a rental property instead of selling it. In any case, they need someone local to take care of both their property and their tenants. That's where you come in.

Your job is to visit the owner's property on a regular schedule, and make sure that it's being maintained: no overgrown lawns, no broken windows, etc. The owner will usually set a schedule for on-premises inspections. You set up an appointment with the renter to tour the inside of the property so you can make sure it's in good repair. Likewise, if the tenants have a problem such as a broken appliance, they need someone local to call to get it fixed.

If something needs to be fixed, you either do it yourself or hire someone to do the repair.

## The Pay

The pay you receive is typically a percentage of the rent that is paid to the landlord, and ranges from 5% to 10% for residential rental properties.

## Training

Typically no formal training is required.

## Licenses Required

Individual municipalities may have requirements, but as far as my research showed, no state or federal licenses are required.

# Getting Started

## Is this for me?

While the job may sound glamorously hands-off, this is not a job you can do entirely from behind a desk, or on regular hours. The day-to-day work can involve a lot of mediation between angry tenants, angry landlords, and sometimes intransigent workmen, so your people skills will be very important here. Staying organized is also essential: tenants and workmen have tight schedules. No one wants to hear "I'll be there sometime between 8am and 4pm", but even worse is someone who makes an appointment and doesn't show up.

If you're someone who doesn't enjoy working with people, or who is always running behind, this is probably not the job for you. On the other hand, if you have strengths in those areas, being a rental property manager can pay quite well.

## Market Research

One thing you'll need to do is get a feel for how many rental properties there are close to you. As you can imagine, there are more in New York City than in rural North Dakota.

Local real estate agents are a great resource for you. They have a good feel for how many rental properties are in a given area, and also how many property managers there are. They'll also know some of the landlords, including what they expect and maybe what they pay. They can also be a great source for referrals, so keep in touch with them.

Presuming there's enough rental property in your area to meet your income needs, you need find out what it's going to take to get the contracts.

## Find the Customers

This is the dreary part, but it's got to be done: you need customers before you can do work for them. A good place to start is your local newspapers: look for "house for rent" advertisements, contact the owner, and ask if they have someone to manage their property. If they do, ask what they like or dislike about the person they use now. Another good source of leads is real estate folks. Many rental properties are houses that the owner couldn't sell at the price they wanted, and they're choosing to keep it and rent it out. Real estate people know these properties very well, so they're a good group to know.

There are also property management companies, who may be looking for employees. This gains you fringe benefits and releases you from marketing, but may not pay nearly as well, since they're paying you out of the same 5%-10% slice, but also paying for your desk, the lights, the phones, the staff, etc.

### Get Paid

This is the easy part. You'll typically be paid by the landlord, monthly. Usually you get a check in the mail, but sometimes it will be a direct deposit in your bank account. The amount from each individual property may not be very much, but they add up quick.

## Getting Good

Word of mouth is vital in this business: one owner telling another that you are reliable, responsible, and professional is worth a lot of cold calls to property owners.

Every dollar counts: the last thing the owner wants is to spend extra money to have a leak fixed or an appliance repaired. If you're in contact with reliable and economical professionals in the area, you're in a position to help the owner save themselves both money and aggravation. You're also in a position to make solid friendships with the local professionals by getting them business. Everyone wins.

It's fairly common for each landlord to have their own contract paperwork. Therefore, it's a good idea for you to have access to a reasonably priced law professional who can look over that paperwork to make sure it's not obligating you to do more than you expect. You don't need to spend a fortune on a lawyer, but it's a good idea to have someone you can go to in a pinch.

## Other Resources

- National Association of Residential Property Managers (NARPM)
- Vacation Rental Manager's Association (VRMA)
- National Property Management Association (NPMA)
- Institute of Real Estate Management (IREM)

# 4
# Locksmith

*Opening Locks without a key, or changing the key that opens them*

You can pick your friends, you can pick your locks, but picking a friend's lock (without their permission) could result in jail time.

## The Pay

The pay ranges from $30/hr for scheduled on-site work, to $45+/hr for emergency on-site work, down to about a dollar for simple key duplication. Re-keying services depend a lot on the brand of lock. Some you'll be able to do on site, others you'll have to order out.

## Training

The basics of locksmithing can be learned from the many books and videos on the subject. Some lock & safe companies will offer classes and even certifications in working with their particular product line. Most of the training you need is simply practice, practice, practice.

## Equipment

### Required

- A key duplication machine
- A set of lock picks
- Simple mechanical & electrical tools

### Good To Have

- An industrial strength drill w/metalworking bits
- A variety of viewing gear (magnifying glass, loupe, flexible fiber scope w/light, etc

## Licenses Required

According to the Associated Locksmiths of America, the following thirteen states and territories require a license to practice locksmithing:

- Alabama
- California
- Connecticut
- Illinois
- Louisiana
- Nebraska
- Nevada
- New Jersey
- North Carolina
- Oklahoma
- Tennessee
- Texas
- Washington D.C.

## Getting Started

### Is this for me?

The work is simple and straightforward, moderately skilled, and in light but steady demand. If you are looking for dawn-to-dusk excitement, this is not the job you are looking for. If, on the other hand, you're looking for steady, manageable part- or full- time work that lets you manage your time and catch up on your reading or television during the slow periods, locksmithing may be the key to a happy life.

### Market Research

Know your market. Locksmithing is a job that everyone needs done once in a while. Houses being bought or sold, apartments and commercial real estate leases being established, all require rekeying by a locksmith. Duplicate keys are a steady demand as well, and the occasional lockout call will come in. Check the yellow pages and see how many people in your area are actively working as locksmiths. Not all that many are required per 100,000 population. If you're in a small town with 10,000 people and there are already two locksmiths in town, either see if you can buy one of them out, or think about a different vocation.

### Get Trained

Online and correspondence courses abound for locksmithing. Local trade colleges probably also offer classes. You can also often get a job working with/ for another locksmith, and pick up the skills you'll need that way.

### Get Your Equipment

Only the key duplication rig and the lock-picking set are locksmith-specific. The rest of your gear is going to be direct from the hardware store.

### Do It!

Waiting for the phone to ring is the worst part. While you're not on the job, try handing out business cards at apartments, home building sites, and commercial real estate agents' offices.

### Get Paid

Mostly you'll get a job request and give the customer an estimate. If they accept, you do the job, count the hours, and bill them as you leave. If you're doing work for a municipality, you may get a voucher or just a notice to pick up your check at the end of the month.

## Getting Good

Practice, practice, practice. All the people I know that work on locks do it constantly, as a way to keep their hands busy: picking locks while watching TV or while they're at their kids' sporting events. Their eyes are on the entertainment, but their fingers are hard at work.

## Other Resources

- Associated Locksmiths of America (www.aloa.org) is a good place to start

- Most states, including Texas, California, Louisiana, Massachusetts, and Tennessee have a statewide association

- Some cities (Philadelphia, for instance) have a citywide organization as well

Belonging to these organizations is a great way to keep up on the changing laws and regulations.

# 5
# Taxidermist

*Real stuffed animals!*

Whether it's for a museum display or a trophy for the wall, taxidermists prepare animals for display. Taxidermy combines carpentry, metalwork, chemistry, and animal physiology to produce fine art.

## The Pay

Taxidermists are paid per completed job. Stuffing a small animal runs $200-$600 all-in, "trophy head" mounts for larger animals run $400-$800, and full-body larger animals run $1000-$1800. Wall-mounted antlers/horn sets run $100-$400, depending on size and type. Most taxidermists also offer hide tanning and skeletal preparation services as well, for people who want to turn their trophy hide into a rug or wall-hanging, or just want to display the skull or skeleton.

## Training

Formal training isn't always required. Lots of people just learn by trial and error. There are plenty of books and videos on the how-to's of taxidermy, and classes as well, although sit-down taxidermy classes are somewhat rarer than welding or dance classes.

## Equipment

Since most taxidermists have their own style and their own methods, a "standard" list of equipment is impossible to produce. Tanning, woodworking, metalworking, sewing, glassworking, some kitchen chemistry, and even beetle-keeping can be involved. At the very least you're going to need a good, solid workbench and a good selection of woodworking and butcher's tools to start.

## Licenses Required

Forty-three states (all states *except* California, Florida, Kansas, New Jersey, New York, South Carolina and Texas) require a license to be a professional taxidermist. Beyond that, the federal government requires a license to stuff migratory birds.

## Getting Started

### *Is this for me?*

There is a lot to being a taxidermist. You're a jack-of-all trades. The work itself requires someone with an artistic eye who is good with their hands, and someone with the patience required for tanning and hide preparation. The business requires someone who enjoys both talking with people and working on animals. If that sounds like you, taxidermy might be a good choice.

### *Market Research*

A lot like Traveling Massage Therapy, there are always a lot of people advertising taxidermy services. The vast majority of them have no current customers while a minority have more work than they can handle. Jobs like this are all about skill and results. The unskilled get washed out quickly, but skilled taxidermists get large amounts of repeat business and a lot of word-of-mouth advertising. Breaking into the market can be difficult, but it is *not* impossible. Expect to spend a lot of time preparing demonstration pieces (and sometimes selling them) and talking with individual hunters and other organizations before you establish yourself as a local professional who gets the job done.

### *Get Trained*

Roadkill. Seriously. Every taxidermist I've talked to started by preserving fallen animals, whether roadkill or "down" animals found in the countryside. There are snippets on youtube, and how-to DVDs, you can ask other taxidermists, take classes, or even apprentice. But in the end, practice makes perfect and roadkill is where a lot of folks start.

### *Get Your Equipment*

As discussed in the equipment section above, there is no hard-and-fast list of equipment. A very short list would include basic carpentry tools for the bases, wire and metalworking tools for the internal structural supports, and a variety of sewing equipment to join and bind the skins. After that, it's really going to depend on your specialty.

*Do It!*

Build up a set of trophy and art pieces to show off your work. Enter them in local contests, have them photographed and distribute the photos. Spend time with local hunters, find out what they need or want that other taxidermists aren't offering. Get business cards made up, have a phone line with an answering machine specifically for your business, and have a professional message on it.

On your first calls, be sure to set up a specific appointment to pick up the carcass or hide. Talk to the customer about how they want it prepared: they're not going to pay you until they're satisfied, and redos will kill your profits. Show up on time, get the work done as advertised, and deliver it on time. If it took you less time than you expected, discount it a bit. Customers love things that arrive early and cost less, and word-of-mouth will get you a lot of business in taxidermy.

*Get Paid*

Traditionally, you get paid when the customer receives their goods. This can be a problem with some customers, who may end up trying to use your home or shop as a storage & viewing facility, but patient phone calls will usually do the trick. Prices do vary by difficulty, so the final amount you charge may be more or less than your original estimate.

## Getting Good

After you master the basics of preparing the animal and building the support structures inside it what's left is mainly art. For all animals, pose is important, as are the eyes. For large full-body pieces, a lot of taxidermists start adding more realism features to the base, like rocks, brush, or even other small stuffed animals. You are building works of art to go in people's homes and businesses, so be as creative as you can.

## Other Resources

- National Taxidermists Association
- Most states, including Illinois, Maryland, Texas, Kentucky, and Iowa, have a state taxidermist association
- Google [Taxidermist association] for more

# 6
# Well Driller

*Get paid to make holes in the ground*

Well drilling is a very specific job: you drill a hole in the ground, at a specific place, to a specific depth, as specified by the customer. Some customers expect to pay for a wet and working well, which you cannot possibly guarantee.

## The Pay

The raw pay is quite good, $10,000 for a single well drilled is quite normal, and you can do more than one a day. On the other hand, your equipment and maintenance costs are also high, so not all of that is profit. Likewise, the work is seasonal, more work in the summer, less in the winter, generally up and down with homebuilding.

## Training

Training is usually on-the-job working for another drill rig operator, although some heavy equipment companies (like those that sell drilling rigs) offer training of some kind, either in person or on DVD.

## Equipment

*Required*

- A drilling rig
- A big selection of bits
- Replacement bits
- Clothes that can take getting dirty

*Good to Have*

Landscaping gear can help preserve the land around your work area. Having an adze to cut a drainage path can save a very expensive flower bed from flooding and earn you substantial brownie points with your customer.

### Licenses Required

Virtually all states require a license to drill for water, often on par with the professional contractors licenses, so you'll probably need to study up for the exam.

# Getting Started

### Is this for me?

You will have to be able to work with the customer to make sure they understand what they're paying for: a hole in the ground. Being clear about this beforehand will let you be firm about it later on. If being firm with an upset customer is something you find hard to handle, this job may not be for you.

Likewise, there is a substantial up-front cost for this business: the drilling rig. Whether you buy it outright or finance it, your drill rig is going to run you tens of thousands of dollars. If you cannot afford to spend that up front, well drilling is not for you.

### Market Research

Getting to know the local homebuilders, contractors, and construction outfits is vital. Make sure there's room in the economy for a well driller before you decide to be one.

### Get Trained

Usually this means working with someone else on similar equipment, since it's not common for heavy equipment to come with much in the way of how-to videos or classes.

### Get Your Equipment

There are new & used drilling rigs available online and in local business auctions. If you go the used route, be prepared to maintain the rig on your own, since there won't be a warranty. As always, shopping around can save you a lot of money.

*Drill!*

A day in the life of a well driller is pretty straightforward: drive to the job site, find out where and how deep they want you to drill, set up your gear and drill. Repeat until the customer is satisfied or has no more money to drill holes.

*Get Paid*

Many factors go into what you charge. You may get paid by the site visited, by the hole drilled, and/or by the foot-depth drilled. Diameter of the hole drilled and what you're drilling through also factor in, since the wear-and-tear on equipment matters as well. You may also provide hole lining, pump installation, pipe, and other additional services, possibly with their own price schedule. A successfully drilled well may easily run over ten thousand dollars before it's operational, and the majority of that will be your services.

## Getting Good

You will get to know your rig a bit too well. The noises it makes when the bit is wrong for the earth you're drilling through, when it's over- or under- torqued, etc. Having the right set of bits for a given locale is important. Whether you want to or not, you're going to become a bit of an expert on local geology. You will also get to know a lot about the permitting process in your area, since making sure the customer is allowed to drill on this property is important.

## Other Resources

Most states, from New York to Nebraska, have a statewide well drilling associations. Georgia, Kentucky, Maryland, North & South Carolina, Tennessee, Virginia, and West Virginia have a combined organization: the South Atlantic Well Driller's Association. You should Google [well driller association] to see what local resources there may be.

# 7

# Traveling Massage Therapist

*Have portable massage table, will travel*

You bring relaxation and wellness to your customers. While a lot of massage customers go to the spa for this service, many companies are now offering on-premises massage as a perq, and there are customers for whom a visit to a spa is inconvenient. Typical massage sessions last 20-30, 50-60, or 80-90 minutes.

## The Pay

Rates vary widely, from $40 to $150 per hour, not including tips.

## Equipment

You should keep in mind that you will be carrying all your equipment to and from the premises, so weight and bulk are important considerations.

### Required

- A portable massage table
- Clean towels/sheets (per customer)
- Hand cleanser (for yourself)
- Surface cleansers (for your equipment between customers)

### Good To Have

- Massage Oils
- Odor neutralizer and/or scent for the room
- Ambient music source with soothing music
- Bottled water (for your customers, after the massage)

*Luxuries*
- Hot towel dispenser
- Free-standing foldable robing screen

## Licenses Required

Forty-four states (all states *except* Idaho, Kansas, Minnesota, Oklahoma, Vermont, and Wyoming) require a license or certificate to be a massage therapist.

## Getting Started

### Is this for me?

Obviously, this job involves touching people. If you're uncomfortable around people of particular races, genders, hairstyles, or whatever, this may not be the job for you. You can reasonably expect your customers to be clean and neat when you arrive, but if scars, hair, moles or such bother you, this may not be the job for you. The job is mildly physical. You will be moving your own equipment, and working physically on other people, so a certain degree of physical capability and strength is required.

If, on the other hand the idea of helping people relax, directly impacting how they will feel today, and improving their mood, muscle tone and mental body model appeals to you, then this will be both mentally and financially rewarding.

### Market Research

This is a bit tricky. In every community I checked, there are a large number of massage therapists available, and the majority of them are underemployed. On the other hand, there always seems to be a minority that have more work than they can handle. It is apparently a case of many people who want to do it, but few people who can do it well. Don't be intimidated if the market looks saturated, there is always room at the top.

A good place to start is at whatever massage school you decide upon. They will usually have an on-premises massage facility with very low prices where you practice. They will also have a referral service, and know what areas of town are good resources for customers.

Don't be afraid to branch out on your own. Visit local businesses which are doing well and ask if they'd be interested in adding a massage perq to their package. Visit local gyms, dojos, and fitness schools and ask if they have a partner program, or whether you can start one with them. Most will not want to commit before you are actually certified, but you can usually figure out whether they're even interested in the first place. If they are, you have an excellent customer base from which to start.

Hotel concierge staff is also a good source of referrals, although it is vital to make a top-notch business impression when dealing with them. They simply can't afford to give their patrons a bad referral, so their trust in your professionalism is vital.

## Get Trained

There are numerous massage colleges out there, shop around. Make sure you're comfortable with the people, staff, and curriculum.

## Get Your Equipment

If there are 100 massage therapy schools, there are 1,000 places to buy the related equipment brand new. Tons of lightly used equipment is for sale in your local newspaper's classifieds, eBay, craigslist, job fairs and flea markets. Take your time and shop around. Buy something you'll be glad you're using… upgrading equipment is more of a pain than buying the right equipment in the first place.

## Work your contacts

Whether you're partnering with gyms, working with businesses, servicing individual clients, or all of the above you'll need to stay in touch with people. Call everyone on a regular basis: at least once a month, just to touch base and remind people you're available. Likewise, until you're fully booked, there is no substitute for getting out and making a few new contacts.

## Massage!

While potentially physically tiring, this is one job you will probably enjoy doing all day long. That said, there are the odds-and-ends that aren't the actual massage, and they can make a big difference in how much your customers appreciate you and thus how much money you make. Professionalism means no rushing in, no rushing out, and certainly never rushing through a massage.

If the 50-minute massage is supposed to start at noon, then you have to remember to arrive early enough to get set up before then. Likewise, allow time to strike your equipment and get it back out to your car.

### Get Paid

If you are dealing serially with individual customers, it's normal to agree on the price and even get credit card information over the phone before you leave. If you are serving a business and will set up one time for multiple customers, the way you get paid may be quite different. You may get paid a flat rate for a number of hours, whether you have bookings or not. If the company is subsidizing the massage, you will usually have to account for that, often getting paid the subsidy at a later date.

If the individual customer is paying anything, that will usually be collected after the massage, as is the case with hair salons and restaurants where a tip is included with the payment.

## Getting Good

Listening to what the customer asks for is pretty easy. Remembering *next* week what they asked for *this* week may be harder. A lot of massage therapists keep a notebook on their regular customers: just a note about prior injuries or current work activities that might be important to keep in mind during a massage.

Another thing to keep in mind is that there is no One True Massage Technique. The more places you go and learn, the more value you bring to the (massage) table, and thus the more you may be able to bill. Remember that most customers want pretty much the same massage every time. Don't fall into the situation where you're trying new things because you're bored. Try new things on family, friends, or other therapists, let the customers get comfortable with a consistent regimen and ask for something different if they want it.

## Other Resources

- American Massage Therapy Association (AMTA)
- The Massage Register www.MassageRegister.com
- www.MassageTherapy.com has lots of information about the field of massage therapy

# 8
# Limousine Driver

*Home, Jeeves.*

Limousines are for more than just the rich and glamorous. They're also for people who want to get their whole family to the airport on time and not worry about parking. They're for tourists who come to town and don't want to drive a car. They're even for the mother whose car is in the shop, but needs to run some errands after work. In short, there's a lot of work out there for people who don't want to "waste" their time concentrating on driving. That's where you come in.

## The Pay

The pay is pretty good. Limousine services charge $50-$250 an hour, depending on the vehicle, duration, and service level. While taxes, gas and maintenance do eat into that, it can still be a very profitable business.

## Training

Whether you need a license or not (see below) it's a good idea to take a professional driving course. They're available from a variety of sources, from specialty limousine driving schools to high-tech tactical driving schools. Sometimes even from the police themselves.

## Equipment

### Required

- A limousine
- A pair of black or grey dress slacks, white shirt, tie, and dress shoes.
- A cellphone and a good (not expensive, good) watch

### Good to Have

- A portable tv/dvd player with family-friendly content to keep the kids occupied and quiet

- Give-away maps to everything everywhere.

- Give-away coupons for everything, everywhere

### Luxuries

- A portable tv/dvd player with *your* favorite content, for the parts of your job that involve you waiting outside in the car.

- A cooler with cold drinks (for your customers)

- Prepackaged snacks (likewise)

## Licenses Required

Some cities such as New York require a taxi (or hack, or hackney) license for limo drivers. The vast majority do not require special licensing. Check with your city hall or local motor vehicle department to find out what the rules are in your area.

It is safe to assume that you'll have to pass a driving test (like your regular driver's license, but in your transport vehicle) and get a background check.

## Getting Started

### Is this for me?

Surprisingly there are lots of kinds of jobs for a limo driver. Because you are your own boss, you can pick and choose. The job is mostly driving and keeping your passengers safe, but it's also a lot of being polite, dealing with noise and occasionally with unruly passengers, and keeping your limo clean. If the traffic, the passengers, or the potentially long waits while they do their shopping or whatever are going to be a problem, this may not be the job for you.

### Market Research

It is *very* hard to tell how well served a given community is when it comes to limousines. Looking through the yellow pages and counting services is not good enough. Some are large full-time operations, and some went out of business six months ago and haven't told the phone company yet.

One good place to check is at the highest-end hotel in your target area. Talk to the concierge, the bellhop, and the valet. Ask them how they're fixed for reliable, clean, prompt limo drivers. If they need more, you're in great shape. If you check with the top 5 hotels and they're all pretty much set, then the area is already well served, and getting started may be a challenge.

## Drive!

So you've got a job. The customer has spent their hard-earned money for a limo, and they probably want the royal treatment. Addressing them with "sir/ma'am/young-lady/young-man" and opening the car doors is cheap for you and pleasant for them. Being sarcastic or insincere is a non-starter. Skip the whole thing if you can't do it honestly. But seriously, learn to do it right. People expect the best when they hire a limo. Drivers that give it to them will get way more business than those who don't.

*Never* make a call on your cellphone while you're driving a customer, whether you have hands-free or not. The customer is paying for your attention, whether they said so or not, and it's offensive to split it. When you're with a customer, don't even use your cellphone at all if you can possibly help it. A rule of thumb is: "If you're within earshot of the customer, only use your cellphone if you'd be willing to stop the service and refund their fare immediately." It's totally fair to expect no tip if you break this rule.

## Get Paid

Very often this is cash, at the beginning or end of the trip. Unlike a taxi, you (usually) won't run a mileage meter, so that's not going to be an issue.

Tips are customary, not mandatory. Accept them graciously if they're offered. Most of the world has no gratuity/tip system at all. A lot of foreign travelers don't even know it's a custom, so don't be offended if one isn't offered. It is probably a case of ignorance rather than intent.

# Getting Good

This has a lot to do with reading people and guessing what it is that your customer wants without them having to ask. Does this guy want his kids distracted? Does this woman prefer quiet or conversation? Getting good at telling the difference will make a difference in your business.

Making notes is a great idea. If you keep a list of people and their preferences and where you drove them last you'll be in a much better position to offer them top notch service. Keeping a log book of your driving is a good business practice anyway. Adding notes on each client is just smart.

A very important thing to keep in mind is that there is a difference between dressing *professionally*, which is good, and *stylishly*, which might not be. Several sources have reported that they were actually turned off by an over-styled chauffeur. Don't dress like a dandy. Slick hair, a fake Rolex, or an over-the-top earring might impress your friends but cost you business. When in doubt, go to a major men's clothier (Nordstrom is *always* a safe bet) and talk to a senior person in the men's suits department. Ask if they've got a minute, and if they do, tell him or her you're looking for a professional look. They'll usually be willing to give you some opinions. Listen to them. They know your customers.

If you find yourself driving more high-profile customers around (the kind that bring bodyguards) you may also want to take additional classes in "defensive" or "tactical" driving, where you actually learn how to get away from bad guys intent on causing your customer harm.

## Other Resources

- *American Automobile Association (AAA)*
- *National Limousine Association (NLA)*
- *Statewide limousine organizations (many states have one)*

# MUNICIPAL SERVICES

*Government Work - Sort-of*

There are lots of things that governments need done in a specific way, but that don't warrant creating a whole government agency (and resultant tax burden) to solve efficiently.

Municipality services are businesses whose primary customers are the government, and who work very closely with that government, but are still independent businesses.

In this section four jobs (Crime Scene Cleanup, Tow Truck Operator, Snowplow Operator , and Animal Control Technician) are lumped into the Municipal Services category. Three of the things that these jobs share are the licensing, getting a contract, and working with government offices (city/county/regional/...)

## Licensing

Licenses are required. City, State, and in some cases Federal licenses may be needed for you to run your business in a specific area. For the most part in these jobs, the licensing is designed to keep you from getting hurt, or hurting others, so the training and certification deal with things like how to handle blood safely and who to notify if you see a large gasoline spill. The classes are harder than aromatherapist and easier than space-shuttle technician. Count on cracking the books to get your license, but renewing it is often fairly straightforward.

Finding out what's required is remarkably easy: look in your phone book for the number for your City Hall. Call and tell them that you're interested in learning about licenses required for the job you're interested in, and they'll usually be able to tell you exactly who to call next.

Or even better, you can do the whole process in person. You're going to be spending a fair amount of time in and around City Hall anyway, so take advantage of your first opportunity to look around and get to know the folks.

## Get on The List

Yes, you could get a tow-truck operator license, buy an ad in the yellow pages, and wait. And doubtless every once in a while, someone would find you in the phone book and give you a call, but not very often. On the other hand, Highway Patrol calls for towtrucks dozens of times every day, so being on their short-list is where the action is. Most of the work you get in municipal services jobs comes from getting contracts with the local government agencies, which usually involves getting licensed, applying for (or bidding on) a contract, and then getting on The List.

The List is handled differently everywhere, but basically it is a short list of contractors in the area that the local government has preapproved for hire. Sometimes it's informal: just a post-it next to the clerk's phone. Sometimes it's very very formal: a computer-monitored usage-weighted round-robin scheduler that insures fair distribution of work across the local industry. The important thing is to get on it, and to check your status on a regular basis. Since this is a little different in every situation, check around with other people in adjacent industries: if you're looking at running a tow truck, ask a water-damage-cleanup guy, if you're looking at crime scene cleanup, ask a commercial landscaper that has a city contract. These sorts of people will be able to give you a good idea of how things work in your area.

One word of caution: It is very very rare that there is a who-you-know aspect to this sort of thing, and that's usually an indication that something is wrong. Be suspicious of people who claim to have the inside track. The process to get on the list should be open and straightforward. If it's not, perhaps you need to look around a bit more.

## Working with City Hall

Working with the government has its pluses and minuses. On the plus side, the work is usually steady, and for the most part routine. On the downside, there's often a lot of paperwork between the job and the paycheck. Things to remember when dealing with City Hall:

- Paperwork rules everything. If you're someone who can't stand paperwork, skip this entire job segment. Seriously, poor penmanship or putting the day and month in reverse order (DD/MM/YY vs MM/DD/YY) can cost you a month or more delay in getting paid, because the paperwork gets kicked back and you have to refile.

- Unlike you, the person behind the counter is not driven by a profit motive. For the most part, he or she makes the same wage whether they're amazingly efficient or glacially slow. Their motivation is not the same as yours, so don't expect your urgency to make much impact on them.

- You will need to budget. As often as not your pay will be delivered as an aggregate check for all of your work over a specified period of time. This may mean you'll get your paycheck 6 weeks after you did the work, or two days from now, depending on the disbursement policy of the relevant government agency.

## Conclusion

These jobs pay well but have significant barriers to entry and require people with very specific skills, which makes them different from most of the other jobs in this book. You need to investigate carefully before you set out on this very profitable path.

# 9
## Crime Scene Cleanup
*Have Tyvek Mask, Will Travel*

It makes sense when you think about it. When a crime is committed, it often leaves a mess. Whether that mess is graffiti or a pool of blood, the property owner wants it cleaned up pronto, and the criminal justice folks want to make sure no evidence is lost. From these competing desires was born the profession of crime scene cleanup.

Your job is threefold: get the property back to its original state, preserve any existing evidence, and report any new evidence you uncover.

## The Pay

Service charge per hour is well in excess of $100. An individual scene cleanup can run $1,000 to $3,000.

## Equipment

*Required*

- Camera
- Tyvek-style body suits & masks
- Biohazard waste bags & buckets
- Vacuum systems: Steam Clean and Shopvac-style
- Industrial strength cleansers, deodorizers, solvents

**Good To Have**

- Dedicated Transportation. The family minivan will not tolerate the sorts of messes your equipment will make.
- A good GPS you can update, so you can get to the job site fast
- Carpentry tools for small-scale restoration work

- Pry-bar, Ladder, Wheelbarrow, Pulleys, and other job site equipment

## Licenses Required

See "Municipal Services"

## Getting Started

### Is this for me?

This job is mildly physical, and many locations you have to get to will not be easily accessible, so it's not a job suited to the physically handicapped. It's also messy (it's a cleaning job) and some of the things you have to clean up, remove, or dispose of will be stomach-turning. People who can't stand strong smells or people who faint at the sight of blood need not apply. Lastly, you'll be working closely with the police. A lot. If your hobbies or history might make this uncomfortable for you, you may wish to reconsider this profession, even though in most cases a criminal record is not prohibitive.

### Market Research

Call your local Sheriff's office, local Police office, and local Highway Patrol office, and see if they need more crime scene cleanup help. Find out if they're working with just one company, or have a list of companies they deal with. Find out what it takes to get on their call list. You don't want to spend the money on equipment and training only to find out they already had more crime scene cleanup folks than they can use.

### Get Trained

The Sheriff, Police, and Highway Patrol offices will all be able to tell you what certifications and licenses you'll need. The most common requirement is something called a Blood-borne Pathogens course, which tells you how to safely handle blood and other body fluids without exposing yourself to diseases that they might carry.

It's likely that you'll have to be fingerprinted, since you will be present at a lot of crime scenes, and being able to exclude your fingerprints early makes it easier for the police.

### Get Your Equipment

Your municipality may have a list of stuff the you're required to have on hand at each crime scene (evidence baggies, etc) so make sure you map out all of their needs. This is a job with a potentially very large up-front cost, so make sure you start with the essentials.

### Get on the lists

Contact every law enforcement office and property manager in your area and make sure they know you're available. Find out how they decide who to call, and make sure you're on their lists.

### Clean Up!

Be prepared. Have your gear ready and your consumables fully stocked at all times. Top-off your supplies after returning from each job.

This is, no fooling, a nasty job. You will see, hear, feel, taste and smell things you wished you hadn't, and you may meet people you probably won't be inviting to your next backyard party. Putting up with these difficulties and keeping a professional attitude is where you earn your money.

### Get Paid

This is a more formal process than a lot of other jobs, since you're (usually) contracting with state and local governmental authorities. Invoices have to be done just so, and submitted before specific dates. Your pay arrives as a check some days later, etc.

## Getting Good

According to my brief research, the most common problem with crime scene cleanup companies is their availability. Crimes happen in all sorts of strange places and all sorts of strange hours. The police prefer to work with people who are available Right Now. Likewise, the city usually prefers to work with people who can deal with paperwork well. The big bucks are often available to people who can also handle hazardous materials: see your fire department about hazmat classes.

Another tip: Shop around. Unlike a lot of other jobs, Crime Scene Cleanup involves a lot of consumables, such as suits, masks, biohazard trash bags, and lots and lots of cleansers. Getting the best possible price on these supplies can make a huge difference on your bottom line, so take your time, and shop around. I know one person who went through the county yellow pages and called every single business listed, asking either if they sold supplies he needed, or could recommend someone who did. This took him the better part of a week of part-time effort, and increased his profit-per-job by almost 20%.

## Other Resources

The only association I could find that dealt directly with crime scene cleanup was the American BioRecovery Association (ABRA).

Amazon.com lists several books with ominous sounding titles such as "The Dead Janitors Club: Pathetically True Tales of a Crime Scene Cleanup King" and "Mop Men: Inside the World of Crime Scene Cleaners" which might be of interest.

# 10
# Tow Truck Operator

*Move the Unmoving*

There are several different kinds of jobs you get when you operate a tow truck.

1. Roadside Emergency (such as a tire blowout on the freeway)
2. Inoperable Vehicle (dead battery in a supermarket parking lot)
3. Tow-away-zone tows (business owner has violators towed)
4. Legal Impound (impound via police request)
5. Emergency Road Clearing (police request to help clear a pileup)

Any or all of these may be required of you, if you want to operate a tow truck in a given municipality.

## The Pay

Just to make things complicated, each of the above jobs may get paid in a different way. You may need to deal with insurers or AAA in order to get paid for roadside emergencies and inoperable vehicles, or you may just have to accept cash or credit card. For tow-away-zone tows, you may have a contract with the company whose parking lot has the zone, which gets you a small residual income, or you may rely fully on the impound-release payments. Legal impounds towing may be a paid job, or may be required, depending on your locality. If you are someone who can't handle keeping a fair number of loose ends tightly tied, this may not be the job for you

## Equipment

*Required*

- A Tow Rig
- Emergency roadside equipment (flares, placards, etc.)
- A portable credit card processing system

## Good To Have

- A friendly smile
- 6v, 12v, (and other) charger / starter rigs
- Jerry Can, Gasoline
- Jerry Can, Diesel
- Pry-bar
- Portable air-driven wrench for those tough lug nuts

# Licenses Required

See "Municipal Services"

# Getting Started

## Is this for me?

Obviously, you'll be working near traffic, and often near traffic accidents. This carries a certain amount of physical danger with it, so you'll need to take that into consideration before choosing this job. The job is somewhat physical, and many locations you have to get to will not be easily accessible, so it's not a job suited to the physically handicapped. It's also messy and in the case of tows done at the behest of the Police, sometimes confrontational. The police will work hard with you to make sure that the confrontation problem is as small as possible.

This job is definitely not for everyone, but if you're the kid whose favorite toy was a Tonka truck, and you're ready to graduate to the big leagues, this can be a lot of fun.

## Get Trained

Depending on your region and specific equipment, you may need a commercial class driver's license.

## Get Your Equipment

Towing rigs come in a huge variety of sizes, shapes, and fittings, and just as large a range of prices. All of them can tow a car with a flat-tire off the freeway. Removing a burned-out-hulk from the bottom of a ravine is a different thing altogether; same with a snowbound 18-wheeler. Picking the gear you want, need, and will make use of is a personal choice, but one that can be very important financially, so figure out what tasks you are most likely to be doing, and choose the right rig.

### Get on the lists

Contact every law enforcement office, truck stop, and gas station in your area and make sure they know you're available. Find out how they decide who to call, and make sure you're on their lists.

### Get Paid

For the vast majority of owner-requested tows, you will be paid by credit card. Have a portable wireless credit-card swiper ready at all times. Keep a backup one with an alternate company if you need to.

For law-enforcement requests, you'll most often be paid by invoice & check on some municipality-driven timetable, so make sure your handwriting is neat and you fill in all the blanks every time: mistakes will put you at the end of the line for next month's pay cycle, and time is money.

## Getting Good

Skill in this job is mostly gained from personal experience: handling jobs over and over, seeing situations that become familiar. It's also good to keep in mind the fact that the people who own the vehicle are having a Very Bad Day, and they're likely to need your attitude to be part of the solution, not part of the problem. Smile, you're getting paid for this.

## Other Resources

- Towing and Recovery Association of America
- Many states, including California, Montana, Missouri, and New Hampshire have statewide tow truck associations.

# 11
# Snow Plow Operator

*Clear the Roads!*

Next to driving the Zamboni on an ice rink, the most fun you can have with an ice-borne truck is a snowplow. There are a few types of work for a typical snowplow driver:

1. Police/Municipality route clearing

2. Private route clearing (private parking lots and access roads)

3. Emergency work (clearing paths to stranded vehicles)

## The Pay

Like the tow truck driver, each of these different jobs gets paid slightly differently: private work may have a retainer, and so may some municipality work. Emergency work is generally paid at the time of service.

## Equipment

*Required*

- A Plow Rig
- De-icing salt, sand
- Bright rig-mounted lights for night & snowfall work
- Snow chains or commercial-grade snow tires

*Good To Have*

- A warm truck
- A citizen's band radio, to report trouble or call for help
- Emergency first aid kit
- Pressure activated warming packs
- Extra antifreeze

## Licenses Required

See "Municipal Services"

## Getting Started

### Is this for me?

This job takes place in the snow. That may have been obvious, but it does involve being out of doors in cold weather, sometimes during snow, sleet, hail, and other inclement conditions. You'll also be sharing icy and snowy roads with people who have less experience than you do, so it can be a little dangerous. If these are a problem, then this may not be the job for you.

On the other hand, you get to play "hero" a little bit: being the first person out after the storm and clearing the roads for the rest of the folks. If this appeals to you, this job can be very rewarding.

### Get Trained

Depending on your region and specific equipment, you may need a commercial class driver's license.

### Get Your Equipment

Like a tow truck, a snow rig can be a very versatile piece of gear. They come in a huge variety of sizes, shapes, and fittings, and just as large a range of prices. Most can clear four inches of snow off a residential street. Taking 2 feet of snow off an in-use highway is a different thing altogether; same with a mall parking lot when the snow has covered all the visual lane markers.

### Get on the lists

Contact every mall, law enforcement office, and homeowner's association in your area and make sure they know you're available. Find out how they decide who to call, and make sure you're on their lists.

### Get Paid

Mostly you will send an invoice and get paid by check. Occasionally you'll get a credit card, cash, or personal check. Be flexible. The easier you can make it for the customer, the more likely you'll be to get repeat business.

## Getting Good

Skill in this job is mostly gained from personal experience: handling jobs over and over, seeing situations that become familiar. Having the right tool for the job is important as well. Contact your customers every now and again and make sure you're covering all their needs. Better to spend some money on additional equipment than to lose a contract because someone else offers a service you can't perform.

## Other Resources

The Snow and Ice Management Association (SIMA) puts out a print magazine, and also runs the www.sima.com and www.GoPlow.com Web sites. Several northeastern states (New Hampshire and Maine included) have Snowplow Rodeos, which have a lot of experienced folks available to answer questions.

# 12
# Animal Control Technician

*Varmints 'R' Us*

## The Pay

The pay is variable, depending on species, location, entrances, number of animals to be caught, etc. A typical visit runs at least $100. You may also bill for your time spent exploring the property while making an estimate.

## Equipment

*Required*

- Various Traps
- Mask, Gloves, Heavy Clothing
- Sunglasses, bug spray, other outdoor equipment

*Good To Have*

- First Aid Kit
- Dedicated transportation

## Licenses Required

See "Municipal Services"

## Getting Started

*Is this for me?*

Handling all sorts of animals, at both the cute *and* the dangerous ends of the spectrum, is required. If you have strong allergies, or are bothered by snakes, spiders, and such, this may not be the job for you. This job is physical, and many locations you have to get to will not be easily accessible, so if you're physically handicapped this may not be a good choice.

## Market Research

Although it's not technically a police job, people often call the police when they have an animal problem, so the police are often pretty up to date on the services available, and the demand for them. Call your local Sheriff's office, Police station, and the Highway Patrol. Ask each how animal control is handled in your area. Find out if they're working with just one company, or have a list of companies they deal with. Find out what it takes to get on their call-list. The ASPCA also gets calls about wild or unwanted animals. Check to see if they may have a to-call list as well, and get on it.

## Get Trained

Because the pests and animals present in an area vary so much, this job is *highly* specific to the area in which you work. That means that there's not much you can learn from classes, but there's a huge amount you can learn from other animal control folks working in your area. Contact them. They'll know about the common jobs that crop up that don't make the paper or result in a call to the police.

## Get Your Equipment

What exactly you'll need varies a lot from location to location. In Minnesota you probably won't need scorpion traps. Alligator restraints won't see that much use in Arizona. Find out (from your customer base) what they most often need help with, and prepare for that. Having some "generic hardware" (zip ties, rope, etc) is also useful, for when you don't have the perfect gear on hand.

## Get on the lists

Contact every retail property, law enforcement office, and homeowner's association in your area and make sure they know you're available. Find out how they decide who to call, and make sure you're on their lists.

## Roundup!

Not all of your jobs will be set-a-trap-and-wait situations. A cool head and a patient spirit will take you a long way in dealing with the more peculiar calls. Never had to deal with a stray herd of milch goats? Don't be afraid to reach out for help and advice. Chances are your county or state has a wildlife department that can help you do the job safely and with minimal stress on the animal, so make use of them.

## Get Paid

The calls for this service come in equal parts from the government themselves (herd of sheep loose on the freeway) or from the citizenry (wild raccoon annoying dogs) so the money arrives from both the government and individual landowners. You're going to need to be flexible on how and when you get paid, so budgeting is going to be important.

# Getting Good

According to my brief research, the most common problem with animal control outfits is their availability. Demand occurs in all sorts of strange places and all sorts of odd hours. The work goes to people who are available when it comes in and can handle the task. The big bucks are often available to people who can handle everything from an ant infestation to a herd of elk loose on a playground.

# Other Resources

- National Animal Control Association
- Texas, Florida, New Jersey, and Kansas, as well as many other states, have statewide associations for animal control professionals.

# PROFESSIONAL CONTRACTING

*Certified, Skilled Craftsmen*

In this section, five Professional Contracting jobs are discussed: Plumber, Carpenter, Electrician, Painter, and Tile & Ceramics Contractor. Four of the things that these jobs share are the Pay, Training & Equipment, Licensing, and Customer flow.

These jobs have a lot of things in common. The rest of this section outlines things they share.

## The Pay

The pay is great. Billing more than $100,000 in a year is not uncommon. Billing twice that is doable. You have bigger expenses than other people, too: transportation, tools, license renewals, etc. Despite that, successful professional contractors can and do make very good money. These are some of the best paying jobs in this book.

## Training

It is not at all uncommon to spend $2,000 or even $10,000 on professional training and basic equipment for these jobs. Licenses need to be renewed and equipment replaced and upgraded. These expenses need to be planned out a year or more in advance, so if you are a person who has trouble keeping a budget, these jobs are probably not for you.

At the bargain-basement end of training are union apprenticeships. Apprenticeships cost very little or nothing, and you will probably make a little money while you learn. An apprenticeship usually involves around 2,000 hours of training and a couple hundred hours of classwork over the course of around 4 years. If you wanted to get out there and start making top dollar before that, apprenticeship may not be the route for you, but if you have no alternatives, this may be your way into the field.

**Important Note:** It's critical that you remember that even if you *did* start your craft in the union/apprenticeship mode, that once you have your training, you are your own business once again. You don't *have* to work for anyone in particular, or take jobs you don't want. This book is about making your own way, so don't let someone else take that from you.

## Licensing

Licenses are required. City, State, and in some cases Federal licenses are required for you to run your business in a specific area. These are not "beauty school" licenses. They can be bring-your-calculator multi-day standardized tests only offered in your city at specific times of the year. You can expect to crack the books each year to keep up with the latest technology in your field and the latest legal requirements for your profession.

Learning about the particular license(s) you need is easy: ask the local people in your field. Visit a local professional in your desired field, and ask them what's required. Meeting with them is going to be part of your market research anyway, so getting to know the locals in your field is killing two birds with one stone.

## Local Code, and Inspectors

In each of these fields, there will be municipal codes that define the locally accepted ways of doing things, including both methods and materials. Every city has their own, so you'll need to stay up to date. One great way to keep up is to get to know the local inspectors. They're the people who work for the city that will be checking your work. Being friendly will *not* let you violate code, but it *will* keep you up to date on the current standards: how they test, when they test, what is a judgment call and what's a specific requirement. Plus every inspector is one more person who knows you're a competent professional, and could be a great reference or source of referrals.

# Equipment

## Safety Gear

The most important gear you'll buy is your safety gear. Eye and ear protection, steel toed boots, hard hats, etc., are all essentials for jobs like these. Buy the very best you can possibly afford, and save your money on wrenches, screwdrivers, and the like.

## Tools & Equipment

All professionals will tell you that you should only ever buy top grade gear when you're replacing: the time and effort saved by having reliable equipment will more than cover its additional expense.

That said, buying starter gear can be made manageably inexpensive if you make the effort to search out the odd bargain. Resources like craigslist and the classifieds in your local papers may have lightly used equipment for substantially less than it would cost in a store. When buying used equipment see if you can take an expert along with you to make sure that what you're buying will actually get the job done until you can afford to replace it.

## Transportation

Regardless of your specialty, a vehicle you use exclusively for your work is going to be very useful early on. It doesn't need to have any special features or be ultra-heavy-duty. A basic van or pickup truck that's exclusively for your business will save you a lot of time and trouble very quickly, not to mention wear & tear on the family minivan.

# Customers

## Getting and Keeping Customers

Ask any person in these fields (especially independents) and they will tell you the same thing: managing your customers is far more important than having the latest certification, gadget, or skill. Finding new customers and maintaining the old ones is the single most important thing for being successful these kinds of jobs.

## Finding New Customers

You might think that after spending all that money on training and equipment that your customers would choose you based on that, but they will not.

Getting out there and finding new customers, whether by attending trade shows, meeting with local builders and property managers, or hunting down referrals from other craftsmen is a substantial part of a professional contractor's work week. Budget time for this in your week, and keep at it, even when you're incredibly busy with paid work: next month's paycheck depends on it.

## Maintaining Previous Customers

You might think that after spending all that money on training and equipment and *then* getting the job done right will assure you of repeat business, but that isn't so either.

Customers can be very finicky, and no one person will satisfy them all. It's up to you to find out who they need you to be, and be that person. If this customer is particular about cleanliness and you leave garbage in his garbage can (rather than taking your trash back out with you) he may not call again regardless of how good a job you did installing his equipment. Just the opposite, other customers can be suspicious of professionals who are too clean. While you may not know ahead of time, paying attention can get you a lot of repeat business.

Likewise, touching base on the phone or by e-mail can be a good thing, provided you don't do it too much. (No one likes junk-e-mail) Keeping up to date on your customers' build-out schedules can get you a lot of business before you even have to compete for it. Stay in touch and friendly with your ex-customers, you never know when more work may come your way.

# Getting Good

In most professional contracting situations, being good is usually defined as:

**Competent Technique + Excellent Interaction**

That means that in many cases your customer usually won't be able to see right off how well or poorly you have done your job; they will just know if it is done. Beyond that, whether you get more business from them depends largely on things like arriving and leaving on time, professionalism, how big a mess you left, etc. Your attitude and how you look can have a huge impact on how much work you get. Pay attention to both, and more money will follow.

## Conclusion

These jobs pay well but have significant barriers to entry and require people with very specific skills, which makes them different from most of the other jobs in this book. You need to investigate carefully before you set out on this very profitable path.

# 13
# Plumber

*Water & Gas transport systems*

I will avoid jokes about low-slung jeans and cut straight to the heart of the matter: the world needs plumbers, and it pays them well. Repairs and upgrades are parts of the business, but new installation in homebuilding or business/industrial areas is also needed.

## The Pay

Most professional plumbers would agree that the hourly wages and service fees for their work are good. Like other professional contracting positions, your overall income depends largely on your ability to get the jobs in the first place, rather than making enough money per-job.

## Training

The training for a plumber can be significant, depending on what you specialize in. Interstate high-pressure natural gas pipelines are a lot different than large scale farm irrigation systems in terms of training and licensing, and both require their own expertise. Residential work is typically at the less-complicated end of the training spectrum.

## Equipment

The basic gear for "residential leak-fixing and dispose-all replacement" doesn't go far beyond a basic toolbox from a hardware store. A plumber's snake, pipe wrenches, and a small sledge hammer will get you a long way. Beyond that, it's going to depend on your specialty. The institution you got your training from will have a good list of starting equipment for the work they've trained you for.

## Licensing

Required in all 50 states. See "Professional Contracting"

## Getting Started

### *Is this for me?*

There are almost as many kinds of plumbing work as there are work sites. Given the variety of kinds of work available it will be hard to get bored. On the other hand, plumbing can involve as many hours of paperwork (before and after the job) as it does plumbing. This job isn't for everyone, but many people love it.

### *Do It!*

Take your time and do it right. You really don't want your customer calling you back tomorrow to fix a leak in the work you did today. Likewise, make sure you're doing what they *want* and not just what they asked for. Doing the work well, and working the way the customer wants you to are key to your success.

### *Getting Paid*

As a professional contractor, you will generally invoice the client, and they will pay you at a later agreed-upon date. Even for emergency service calls, payment-on-completion is rare.

## Other Resources

- The Plumbing Web, www.PlumbingWeb.com has a very comprehensive list of resources available for plumbers.
- Virtual Plumber www.VirtualPlumber.ca has a great list of equipment used for various plumbing jobs
- Plumbing Heating Cooling Contractors Association (PHCC)
- Several states, including Indiana, Louisiana and Oregon, have their own statewide plumber's association.
- Some cities (Chicago, for instance) have a local one as well.

# 14
# Carpenter

*Housing and more*

While carpentry may be the lowest paying of the professional contracting jobs discussed here, it also has the most consistent demand. Almost all housing in the US is timber framed, and even in the worst economies there is usually work to be found, in repairs, upgrades, or new construction.

## The Pay

Like other professional contracting positions, your overall income depends largely on your ability to get the jobs in the first place, rather than making enough money per-job. Because this is true across all of the contracting jobs, carpentry, with its lower hourly pay but larger overall demand, tends to keep pace with those other fields.

## Training

The training for a carpenter can be significant- or not, depending on what you do. House-framing is very specific: do it to code or don't do it at all. You will need to know the local code before you even start. Installing crown molding or a new set of cabinets is something a non-professional can do, so it's sufficient to just follow the instructions and obey the measure-twice-cut-once mantra of all carpenters. If you're doing custom detail/relief/carving work, then your training is mostly practice, practice practice. As always, you need to know how to use your equipment safely, so read the manual.

## Equipment

The equipment for "residential wall framer" is pretty simplistic: hammers, saws, etc. Beyond that, the equipment required varies widely in this field depending on your specialty.

## Licensing

Required in all 50 states. See "Professional Contracting"

## Getting Started

### *Is this for me?*

Carpentry is not for everyone. It can be frustrating to get a "knock it out quickly" job if you're someone who loves detail work. Likewise, a customer who wants their crown molding or hardwood cabinetry *just so* may be frustrating for someone whose focus is on volume. The good news is that you can run your business any way you want to. Be honest with yourself and your customers about your areas of expertise, and you'll get as much business as there is to be had.

### *Do It!*

Remember "DIRTFT": Do It Right The First Time. You do not want to get called back to redo work you billed for yesterday. It costs you time, earns you no money, and irritates the customer. The two key things to getting a happy customer and a good reference are doing the work well, and working the way the customer wants you to.

### *Getting Paid*

Carpenters and painters, more so than other jobs in this section, need to be flexible in how they get paid. A lot of the time you'll run things the same way as the other contractors: invoice the customer, and receive payment later. For some kinds of carpentry jobs, however, you'll need to be able to take cash or a check directly from the customer when the work is deemed "complete".

## Other Resources

The National Bureau of Labor Statistics lists these:

- Associated Builders and Contractors : www.TryTools.org
- Associated General Contractors of America, Inc: www.agc.org
- National Center for Construction Education and Research: www.nccer.org
- National Association of Home Builders, Home Builders Institute: www.hbi.org

# 15
# Electrician
*Power Distribution*

One thing which stayed pretty much constant through the recent economic downturn was that every business consumed more electrical power each year than it did the year before. Whether in northern Virginia or southern California, virtually every business is straining the limits of its local power distribution system. That's where you come in.

Even while new construction slowed, the demand for electrical upgrades in existing buildings increased, and that meant work for electricians.

## The Pay

Electricians' hourly wage is as good as any of the professional contracting positions discussed here. Like those other jobs, your overall income depends more on your ability to get the jobs in the first place, rather than making enough money per-job, so remember that how the client feels about your work may end up being at least as important to your income as the job you actually did.

## Training

The training for a electrician can be significant, and there are a lot of sub-specialties and additional certificates you may want to get. There are also a lot of local standards to know, how things have to be done. There may be more study to become an Electrician than for any other profession in this book.

## Equipment

The up-front gear for basic house wiring is not particularly expensive, but the specialty gear for more sophisticated work can be very pricey. This can make early specialization less profitable than it might seem.

## Licensing

Required in all 50 states. See Professional Contracting

## Getting Started

### *Is this for me?*

An electrician is a specialist, and a valuable one. There's a lot of work that has to be done a certain way, and no other way, to meet building codes. If you are a person who has difficulty staying interested or on-task, or sometimes skips steps just to get something working, this may not be the job for you.

### *Do It!*

1. Remember that every electrical call is different, and while you want to do things "exactly right", the customer defines what that means. If this is an emergency fuse blowout, then priority one is getting the customer's lights back on quickly. Whether you continue from there to finish the repairs, or schedule a follow-up during normal business hours to get everything back to full working order should be the customer's choice

2. As an electrician, your impact on the customer can be pretty big. Not just the mess, but also the time with the power off and that spent digging in walls and ceilings while you work can be lengthy and widespread. Minimize your time-and-space footprint as much as you can. The customer will appreciate it.

3. Test everything thoroughly before calling a job "done". Getting called back to fix your previous fix will kill your profit, so check and double-check before you leave the first time.

### *Getting Paid*

As a professional contractor, you will generally invoice the client, and they will pay you at a later agreed-upon date. Even for emergency service calls, payment-on-completion is rare.

## Other Resources

- National Electrical Contractors Association (NECA)
- Independent Electrical Contractor Association (IECA)
- Western Electrical Contractors Association (WECA)

There are also various state- and city- wide organizations as well.

# 16
# Painter

*Upgrade/Redo/Refurb*

Ask any homebuilder, house flipper, or commercial real estate agent what costs they always budget for in a project, and repainting is almost always in the top two. Watch the hardware store commercials, and it won't take long to realize that painting is one of the things most people have trouble doing for themselves. Professional painters are seldom short of work.

## The Pay

Painters' hourly wage, like that of a carpenter, is on the lower end of the professional contractors' spectrum, but it still pays quite nicely. Also like carpentry, the demand is steadier and the market will support more painters in a given area than it will high-power-rated electricians or gas pipeline maintenance people. As always, your overall income depends more on your ability to get the jobs in the first place, rather than making enough money per-job, so remember that how the client feels about your work may end up being at least as important to your income as the job you actually did.

## Training

The training for a painter is pretty straightforward. It generally does not take as long as for other contracting positions, and it's mostly on-the-job, so you're earning while you learn.

## Equipment

The equipment required varies widely in this field depending on what your specialty is. Regardless of your specialty, chances are you will need a dedicated vehicle fairly early, probably a van or pickup truck.

## Licensing

See "Professional Contracting"

## Getting Started

### *Is this for me?*

This job, more so than the others in this section, has a significant aesthetic aspect to it. It's not just "make that wall red", but "make that wall a deep red that compliments this carpet in natural light, and give it a dry-brush finish". That is *not* a definitive or deterministic request, so if you are someone that needs well-defined tasks to be happy, this is definitely not the job for you.

### *Do it!*

1.  All contracting jobs involve a certain amount of "measure twice cut once" mentality, but this is very important for painters. One frighteningly common problem is actually painting the wrong wall, or (on larger jobs) using the wrong color in the wrong place. Take the time you need to get the job done right. It will pay off in the end.

2.  Bring (and use) more drop cloths than you think you'll need.

3.  Do the painting you planned

4.  Mark the areas where there's wet paint

5.  Where possible, talk to the customer before you leave to remind them of things like which walls are wet, when the paint fumes will clear, and how to clean the things you've painted.

### *Getting Paid*

Like carpenters, painters need to be flexible in how they get paid. A lot of the time you'll run things the same way as the other contractors: invoice the customer, and receive payment later. For some other work, you'll actually get paid at the time you complete the work, usually by cash or check.

## Getting Good

On a wall paint-job that's going to last for 10+ years, the customer will eventually notice every uneven brush stroke or paint drip. And they will associate it with *you*. Being very careful about the quality of your work will get you a lot more repeat business.

Unlike the work done by an electrician or plumber, *your* work will be in the customer's view for years to come. Remember that. In jobs like this, the quality of your work comes from your body and your mind, so if you're jittery from too much caffeine, or fuzzy because of lack of sleep, your work *will* suffer.

Working the way the customer wants you to is a wholly different thing, but just as important: showing up on time, being (and staying) clean, and leaving no mess are going to contribute to your reference every bit as much as the fact that you do excellent work. Neglect either your quality or your image, and your reputation will suffer.

## Other Resources

Painters, as a profession, seem to be more often lumped in with interior designers than with electricians, and their associations are usually more focused on the former. Google around a bit and look for something that might meet your needs

# 17
# Tile & Ceramics Contractor

*What IS grout, anyway?*

Chipped countertops, cracked floor tiles, and broken pavers are only the beginning. In every residence and commercial building there are a huge number of ceramic surfaces. Virtually every house-flip, remodel, or rebuild requires the services of a professional "tile guy".

## The Pay

Like most jobs in this section, the pay is very good. $40-$100/hr is very doable. Specialists, as always, command higher wages.

## Training

Training for tile & ceramic work is much like training for carpentry: a lot of your learning is on-the-job, although there are certificates (usually offered by the manufacturers) for all kinds of specialty materials

## Equipment

The equipment required varies widely in this field depending on what your specialty is. Regardless of your specialty, chances are you will need a dedicated vehicle fairly early, probably a van or pickup truck.

## Licensing

See "Professional Contracting"

## Getting Started

*Is this for me?*

Along with plumbing, this is one of the more physical jobs in this section. There's a lot of sitting, standing, scrunching, lying down, and transitions between all of these. If you have a bad back, this may not be the job for you. Likewise, a lot of this work happens in bathrooms and kitchens, so if the occasional "off" odor is going to be an issue, steer clear of this job.

## Do It!

The work varies enormously, so there's no hard outline for how to do a tile job. That said, you will score more points (and get repeat business) if you show up on time, minimize your mess and time on site, and touch base with the customer to make sure they're satisfied just before you leave.

## Get Paid

This is almost always done with invoice-and-check. Rarely will someone want to pay you cash, or with a credit card. When you *do* get the rare cash payment, be *sure* to record it just the same as you would normally, and get that data to whoever is doing your taxes. Defensive paperwork can save you a lot of grief if it turns out that the person hiring you is playing it fast-and-loose with his accounting.

# Getting Good

Unlike a plumber or electrician, your work will be directly in the customer's eye for years, so the visual appeal of your work counts. In jobs like this, the quality of your work comes from your body and your mind. If you're off your mental game, your work *will* suffer. With a counter-top that's going to last for 10+ years, the customer will eventually notice every slight misalignment in the tile, and associate it with *you*. Since you will have far less time to notice your mistakes than the customer will, you will do better if you are hyper-careful about your work.

Working the way the customer wants you to is just as important. Showing up on time, being (and staying) clean, and leaving no mess are going to contribute to your reference every bit as much as the fact that you do excellent work. Neglect either your quality or your image, and your reputation will suffer.

# Other Resources

- Ceramic Tile Institute of America (CTIOA)
- Tile Council of North America (TCNA)

Some regional and statewide organizations also exist.

▼

# FORAGING

## What is Foraging?

Foraging, generally speaking, is the gathering of some desired raw material for sale to someone else. This section describes four jobs (Worm Fiddler, Gold Panner, Marine Logger, and Meteor Hunter) in the Foraging category.

## The Working Environment

Foraging jobs are generally solitary or small-group efforts conducted in the outdoors.

## The Pay

Foraging jobs have extremely variable pay, because some days you will gather more than others. That means that if you need to meet very specific and stable income targets, the jobs in this section are probably not for you.

## Claims and Collecting

**Never** collect from a property before you are absolutely sure you have legal permission to do so. Whether this is staking a claim with a state agency, getting an exclusive lease to gather, or just an informal handshake, you *must* check for permission ahead of gathering. The legal punishments can be very severe, and the law is massively on the side of the people managing the land.

Staking a claim (for mineral collection or marine logging) is both easy and cheap, usually taking a single trip to a state-run office. Mineral claims fees run around $140 per year in California and Nevada, but considering the value of having exclusive access to the resource, that's cheap. The paperwork is simple, the process easy.

## Alternative Foraging Targets

Here are some other things that can be foraged for money, although I couldn't recommend trying to make your living at it.

| Name | What is it | Where/How Found | Who buys it | Value |
|------|-----------|-----------------|-------------|-------|
| Ambergris | Whale Excrement | At the seashore or floating on the sea | Perfumers, Curiosity Shops | $1000+ per ounce |
| Truffles | A tree-root fungus | On roots of certain trees, by trained dogs or trained pigs | Grocers / Herbalists | $300+ per pound |
| Meerschaum | Sepiolite. A soft white mineral chemically similar to talc | Floating on the Black Sea | Professional figure carvers and pipe makers | Highly variable |

## Conclusion

Almost everyone can appreciate the thrill of found wealth. Who hasn't taken joy in finding a coin on the street? There is a broad satisfaction to be found in the "go and get it and bring it back" jobs in this section, and it can be very fulfilling for the right sort of person.

# 18
# Worm Fiddler

*Sell bait to bait shops*

Bait shops provide fishermen with worms, grasshoppers, fish eggs, and a variety of other organic products which fishermen hope will tempt more fish onto their hooks. Those bait shops have to get their bait somewhere, and since bait goes bad fairly rapidly, they need a steady supply. That's where you come in.

Worms used for fishing bait normally live their life between 2 and 8 inches below the surface of the soil. The job is simple: go out into the woods or a field where there are (probably) a lot of worms, "fiddle" them to the surface, pick them up, and sell them to bait shops. Usually this job is done by two people, who divide the fiddling from the picking up, sometimes switching off between the two.

## The Pay

Bait shops will often pay 5 to 10 cents for a bait worm. $12/hr would be 250 worms an hour, or 4 worms per minute. That is very doable. People who get good at this have been known to gather thousands of worms per hour, although that's not a typical person or a typical day.

## Training

Almost anyone can do this. No formal training is necessary, and kids under 10 and their great-grandparents can both do this job.

## Equipment

### Required

- A Stob

  This is simply a wooden stake 1-2 inches across and about a foot long. You can make one yourself from any broken furniture, torn off branch, or kindling wood you have nearby. Cost: probably free.

- A Rooping Iron

  This is a piece of non-polished hardened steel around 18 inches long, as wide as your Stob, and about a quarter-inch thick. Think of a really whopping big wood file (although a wood file would probably be too rough). Most worm fiddlers just get a piece of scrap iron from a junkyard. Cost: < $20US

## Good To Have

- A good pair of heavy jeans
- Water-resistant walking shoes/boots
- Gardening kneepads (usually waterproof)
- 5-gallon painter's bucket with a lid (to hold the worms)

# Licenses Required

As far as I can tell, there is no license required in any state for this activity. However, you probably need permission from the owner of the land you're gathering on, which *may* come from the state, if you're using public areas.

# Getting Started

## Is this for me?

Worm fiddling is definitely an outdoor thing, and it's (lightly) physical. If you're agoraphobic, don't like walks in the park, or are grossed out by the idea of handling worms, this probably isn't for you. The fiddling job is mostly done on your knees, and the gathering job is usually done bent over at the waist, so if you're physically handicapped or have knee or back problems, this probably isn't for you.

You may have a partner, but it's still your own business.

## Market Research

The point of this is to get paid, so the first thing you need is someone who will buy worms. There are three main buyers of worms: Bait / Fishing Supply Shops, Plant Nurseries, and (sometimes) people who do composting. Call local fishing stores and ask if they would be interested in another local supplier of bait worms. They can tell you what kind of worms they want, what they pay, and how many they need per day/week/month.

Each business will in essence be telling you how much they'd pay you per week, if you had all the worms they wanted. If there's one giant bait shop that'll buy $5,000 worth of worms a week, you're in great shape. More likely, you'll have more than one customer who will buy some each week. Your goal is to get enough customers that you can earn however much you want.

## Find places to hunt

Loose, damp soil is where worms live. If you live in the Mojave desert, or in the downtown area of a big city, it'll probably be a long drive to anywhere you might be able to gather worms. Otherwise, just look around: Fields, Greens, Parks, Woods, what-have-you. If you're even remotely near suburbia, or (even better) in a rural area, you've probably got access to worms.

## Fiddle!

1.  Reconnoiter

    The first step is just walking around the area. You're looking for nice, damp soil, probably with lots of grass, leaves, and assorted plants all over. Good worm soil is usually a little spongy, so if you're walking on clay or sand, you're in the wrong spot.

2.  Set the Stob

    Push the wooden stake, pointy side down, into the ground a bit, then pound it in with the Rooping Iron until it's set firmly in the ground. If it wobbles at all, it's probably not in deep enough.

3.  Place the iron

    Kneel down with your knees set on either side of the stob, or perhaps just a bit in front of it. Take the rooping iron, one end in each hand, and lay it flat against the top of the Stob.

4.  Roop

    Press the iron, hard, against the top of the stob, lower one side of the iron, (left or right, it doesn't matter) and while keeping a steady pressure on the Stob, move the iron toward the side you lowered. When you get it right, the Stob will vibrate with a growl or grunting sound. That vibration is going to drive the worms to the surface. A roop usually lasts a little under a second, and you probably roop every second or two. When your knuckles reach the stake, pick up the iron, set it again, and repeat.

5. Gather

   After a few minutes of fiddling (worms are not known for their speed) the worms below the ground within 3 to 10 feet of the Stob will begin to surface. The next step? Pick them up and put them in a handy bucket, sack, or what-have-you.

6. Move and Repeat

   When it looks like you've got all the worms in the immediate area, pull out your Stob, move 5-10 yards, and start over. Repeat until your containers are full, or you're wealthy.

### Get Paid

Your buyers probably want worms in specific quantities, like "baggies of 20 worms" or "buckets of 500 worms", or something similar. It's important that you do this part right, because this is where you actually get paid. Make sure your counts are accurate, that the containers and worms are right, and that everything is well labeled and *clean to the touch* when you go to sell your worms. The customer will appreciate it, and your pay depends on them buying your worms again and again.

## Getting Good

In worm fiddling, it's all about two things: location and technique. Location is fundamental because if there are few or no worms in the soil to begin with, you're not going to have a good day.

There are actually a lot of businesses and organizations, including farms, parks and the like, which depend on worms. Because of this, your county agriculture office probably has a bunch of free data on local worm populations. No, really, they probably do! Look in your phone book for county or state offices, and check under agriculture. Also check with the local fishing/composting/plant-nursery places and find out if they know where there are good places to look for worms.

Technique varies widely, but has a lot to do with how deep and firmly you set the Stob, and getting the vibrations from the iron right. One thing to keep in mind is that you're going to get tired, and that will affect the frequency, strength and duration of the vibrations.

## Other Resources

- State and local worm fiddling (sometimes called "worm grunting" or "worm charming") clubs.

- There are worm fiddling contests, some have even been broadcast on ESPN

- There are videos on YouTube

# 19
# Gold Panner
*Gather the oldest valuable metal*

Gold is for more than just jewelry. Industries of all kinds, from dentistry to semiconductors to auto parts manufacturers, use huge amounts of gold to make their products. There are lots of public places in California, Nevada, Arizona, and Alaska where you can just drive up to a riverbank, put on some boots, whip out your pan, and keep what you find, but places like that don't often yield much gold.

The better places are a bit more remote, and may require you to stake a claim. Surprisingly, there's a very large amount of land out there under the jurisdiction of the US Bureau of Land Management where staking a claim is as easy as paying the $140 filing fee, and marking the claim itself. Thereafter, you are entitled to exclusive use of the land, exclusive rights to all its mineral wealth, and assorted other goodies like the right to sleep & camp there.

## The Pay

As of the writing of this chapter spot gold is worth $1410 per ounce. The words spot, ounce, and gold are all defined very carefully:

> **Spot** means (roughly) delivered to the customer within 2 days.
>
> **Ounce** means a *troy* ounce. That's 32-and-a-bit grams, which is slightly more than the 28-and-a-bit grams that go into a regular ounce of something. These are both different than a liquid ounce, which is part of a cup, pint, or gallon.
>
> **Gold** refers to .999-fine gold

All this means is that making the most money for your time requires slightly more complicated than taking a postal service scale, weighing baggies full of gold dust, and selling it.

## Training

No formal training is needed. People of all ages pan for gold.

## Equipment

*Required*

- A pan - This is typically a shallow wide-bottomed pan or bowl, with ridges around the sloped edges
- A magnet - This is used to separate out the black sand left in the bottom of your pan, leaving the gold dust
- Water-resistant walking shoes/boots
- A scale that measures to the tenth of a gram

*Good To Have*

- A good pair of heavy jeans or waders
- 5-gallon painter's bucket with a lid (to hold water & gravel)

## Licenses Required

None, but you will probably need to stake one or more claims, so learning the specifics of that process will save you a lot of time.

## Getting Started

*Is this for me?*

Panning and its related activities are mostly done in ankle-high water bent over at the waist, so if you're physically handicapped or have knee or back problems, this probably isn't for you. Gold panning is somewhat physical, and it definitely requires some patience. If you want a measurable reward every five minutes/hours/days, you'll want to do something else.

*Market Research*

Gold is was, and always will be valuable, so this may be the only job in this book where no market research is necessary.

*Find a buyer*

Gold is beautiful, but you can't eat it.

As easy as you would *think* it might be to sell gold, it's not. You'll want to check around your area as well as the towns nearest your panning location to see who's buying gold, and on what terms. Jewelers and Coin Dealers often buy gold, or know who does. Ask about their requirements. Will they take dust? Nuggets? Prices will vary based on questions like that. Be prepared: have backup buyers.

## Find places to Pan

Another of the things about this job that is unique within this book is that you probably shouldn't waste your time looking up where to go or what to buy on the Internet. There are far more people out there selling bogus maps and overpriced equipment to gullible would-be gold miners than there are useful Web sites devoted to helping people actually succeed.

Physical locations to start panning include tourist sites hosted by the state or city in which the gold can be found. These are great places for three things: practicing your panning, honing your patience, and meeting people. They are *not* great places for profitable gold panning, since the yield per hour will be very low. Meeting the people in the area, though, can be quite useful. They may have tips about places to pan, or pointers to people who are more serious about gold panning.

## Get Your Equipment

Getting a basic outfit pack is as easy as visiting a gold panning tourist trap and buying what's on the shelf.

## Stake a Claim

You can skip this step while you're working public panning sites, but to make real money you'll need exclusive access to the area. This means either working your own claim or working one leased from another claim holder.

## Go for the Gold!

Panning for gold is mostly a matter of letting gravity and friction separate the gold from the mud.

1. Trowel gravel and sand into the pan
2. Add water for rinsing the dirt.
3. Slosh the pan in a circular motion, letting the muddy water slosh out a bit at a time

4. Pick out any large rocks.

5. Add more water, rinse, repeat.

Eventually you end up with "heavies", "heavy sand", and/or "black sand" along with gold dust at the bottom of the pan. Which you get depends on where you're panning. Once you're down to gold dust and black sand, you can use a magnet to gently remove the sand, and you're left with the gold dust.

Some people recommend using mercury to extract the gold from paydirt. Unless you know all the legal and health hurdles, don't do it. Mercury use is legally prohibited in most areasand mercury vapor is highly toxic. It's probably a bad idea to do this regardless of your situation.

### Get Paid

You get paid by the weight and purity of the gold you bring in to your buyer. Given that you can carry a lot of gold, it's best to spend as much time in the field as possible, and only make your sale when you've got a full pouch.

## Getting Good

Sometimes, it's about finding what others miss. Many a time an old pro will work a claim that's been worked before, only to find plenty of gold with a more practiced eye and hand.

Some knowledge of geology is also very useful, particularly when it comes to tracking stream beds, both wet and dry. Knowing where bedrock starts and the relative density of the various rocks in the area can make the panning process easier to plan and execute.

## Other Resources

- Bureau of Land Management
- State Mineral Resources Board
- Gold panning organizations

# 20

## Marine Logger

*SCUBA and Lumberjacking: Together at last!*

Marine loggers gather timber from underwater sites

There are two major areas for underwater (salvage) logging in the United States: the Great Lakes for old growth timber, and the Gulf Coast for cypress timber. A third way to make money underwater logging is harvesting trees covered by the creation of reservoirs or lakes, but this section is primarily about the first two.

## Great Lakes Old Growth Timber Salvage

So-called "old growth" timber is prized for its narrow growth rings and very hard texture. Unfortunately for modern logging, the warmer climate and larger intra-tree spacing doesn't yield the same density wood as was once harvested from North America. Furniture builders in particular will pay high premiums for old-growth timber, whether in log or cut & finished state.

During the 18th and 19th centuries, logging was a huge industry in the great lakes area, and a lot of the old growth timber harvested from the surrounding parts of the northeast was transported by floating the cut logs downstream in huge rafts, to be collected later and brought to the major port cities. During this process, a small but significant percentage of the logs became waterlogged and sank to the bottom of the cold, still waters of the great lakes. The cold water has preserved those logs in almost perfect condition, and individual logs worth thousands, or even into the tens of thousands, of dollars, lie on the bottom of the great lakes and its tributaries today. Recovering these logs and selling them can be very profitable

## Gulf Coast Cypress

Cypress swamps are protected water habitats, and it is illegal to cut down cypress trees just about everywhere. Cypress wood however, is still much in demand, and the timber industry pays a high premium for it.

In most cases it is illegal to fell a cypress, but it can be perfectly legal to harvest cypress trees that have fallen naturally and sunk to the bottom of their swamps. Scouting and harvesting these trees is a profitable business.

## The Pay

Like the other jobs in the Foraging chapter, the pay is highly variable: the classic boom-and-bust feast-or-famine. Individual logs or trees can be worth $5,000 to $15,000, so a weekend's effort that returns two or three targets can be quite a payday. On the other hand, SCUBA gear, diesel fuel, and food for the crew cost real money, so the trips where you get nothing will set you back substantially.

## Training

This is arguably the most hazardous profession in this book, so don't take your training for granted. Consider going out with an existing company or crew for a season to get a feel for the job, its pay, and its dangers.

The reason I didn't include "learn to SCUBA dive" here is because if you don't already have hundreds of dive hours under your belt, this profession would be almost suicidal. This is definitely not for beginners.

## Equipment

### Required

- SCUBA gear

  This is not your weekend-dive project, so expect to lay out additional money to buy some specialty equipment.

- A boat with industrial capabilities

  This is not your weekend boating excursion either. You'll need hauling equipment, tank refilling, etc.

- Logging & Timber Transport Gear

  Not many jobs require a scuba tank and a chainsaw, but this is one of them. Likewise once you get your treasure to land, you'll still need to deliver it to the mill or yard who bought it.

*Good To Have*

- Several Strong Partners/Coworkers

## Licenses Required

SCUBA license required. Some areas have lumber-gathering licenses as well. Some areas require claims to be filed as well.

## Getting Started

*Is this for me?*

Unlike most jobs in this book, this is definitely not a single-person enterprise: you will want a team for this. Why? Well SCUBA diving without a buddy is stupid all by itself, but the physical work required to wrestle dead trees out of the mud, float them to the surface, prep them for travel, and haul them to the end consumer is also a non-starter for most people less well built than Hercules.

*Market Research*

In this particular case, Market Research is absolutely essential. The market for water-soaked rare timber is quite small, so you must find a list of potential buyers before you set out. Specialty wood vendors are a good place to start: find out where they buy from, and follow upward in the chain until you find someone who is interested in buying what you're gathering. Get terms and conditions up front, since you're going to be doing a lot of work and laying out a fair amount of cash before you bring in your first timber.

*Get Your Equipment*

Chainsaws, hoists, wetsuits, wood drying kilns. You are going to need a lot of very unusual equipment in this field, and a lot of it is very expensive. Shop around, but don't buy anything that isn't good quality. There are lots of ways to get hurt SCUBA diving, even more in logging. Together, you're an insurance company nightmare, so make sure you're taking good care of yourself when you get your gear.

### Stake a Claim

For great lakes timber salvage, you actually stake a claim with the state land management outfit. Similar requirements may exist for gathering sunken cypress.

### Work the claim

1. Search for logs (visually or with sonar)
2. Dive to validate your find
3. Float the logs
4. Haul them to shore
5. Prepare them as required by your contract
6. Transport them to the buyer

### Get Paid

How you get paid is really up to your buyer. That said, checks and cash are the more common options.

## Getting Good

Professionals may tell you there's a lot of intuition, guesswork, and gut-feel in this job, and to a point, that's true. But you *can* take a lot of the "luck" out of the job by doing diligent research on where you stake your claims and how you sell your logs. Check historical claims and talk to locals: is this area heavily worked? Check with multiple sawmills to find out who wants what kind of logs. Some want a minimum of so-many inches, others are happy with saplings. As with every business, if you take the time to match buyer and product carefully, you'll do well.

## Other Resources

I could not find an association or Web site of any size dedicated to this business specifically, but the United States Bureau of Land Management has plenty of resources. Check out their Web site: www.blm.gov.

# 21
# Meteor Hunter

*All this from a magnet on a stick.*

The image of the meteor crater in Arizona is well known around the world, but meteor strikes of that size happen only a few times in hundreds of thousands of years. But tens of thousands of times an hour, all over our planet, tiny flecks of space rock plunge into our atmosphere. Most of them are the size of grains of sand, and burn away into hot gas long before they reach the surface of the earth. Most of the rest, when they land, are just tiny grains of black sand, almost invisible to the naked eye, and virtually worthless. But meteorites (chunks of extraterrestrial rock pea-sized and larger) can be worth tens, hundreds, or even thousands of dollars.

Like most foraging jobs, there are a lot of people who do it as a hobby. Professionals are few and far between, and tend to keep their distance from the hobbyists. Professional meteor gathering can be an expensive endeavor, and good hunting areas are carefully guarded secrets.

## The Pay

This is possibly the most difficult aspect of meteor hunting: turning your finds into money. Meteors are, after all, rocks. There are lots of rocks on planet earth that are not meteors, and non-professionals (who make up the bulk of the buyers & market) have a difficult time differentiating between the reals and the fakes. It's a little like buying antiques: a substantial part of the value comes from the provenance and reputation of the locater and seller. Building a reputation as a reliable meteor hunter (and potentially seller) depends on a consensus of respect in the community and time. Neither can be established immediately.

## Training

Almost anyone can do this. No formal training is necessary- kids do it. That said, the successful meteor hunters spend a large fraction of their time researching where to go compared to actually going there. A lot of your success will hinge on contacts you make and data you gather.

# Equipment

## *Required*

1. Magnet-on-a-stick

   The traditional tool of the meteor hunter is a walking stick with a powerful magnet near the foot. The walking stick is used to ease the effort of the (long) hikes that are a part of the professional meteor hunter's life, and the magnet is used to find out if a surface rock is ferric (iron-based, and magnetic).

2. Metal Detector

   Not all meteors are lying right on top of the ground. The older the fall (and the heavier the meteor) the more likely the meteors are to be subsurface. Metal detectors are virtually essential for hunting these down.

3. An extremely reliable off-road vehicle

   Many of the locations you're going to be visiting are remote, and getting there is going to be a challenge all in itself. Don't add "vehicle failure" to your worries.

4. A reliable GPS

   Keeping hyper-accurate records of where each meteorite was found is very useful to the scientists who study meteors, and just as useful to you for establishing where to look. You won't be successful without one.

5. Portable computer

   You're going to want to reference maps, make notes, calculate trajectories, and (when you're in town and connected) send e-mails, beam pictures, and download research. A computer is a must-have in the field

## *Good To Have*

1. A backup GPS (maybe two)

   Really. Lots of things go wrong when you're four hours' drive from the nearest town, and twelve hours from the nearest electronics store. This goes for metal detectors and computers too.

2. Spare batteries for everything

   All of the above goes triple for batteries. You're bringing a lot of electronic gear into the field, and it's just that much dead weight if it's not powered.

3.  Camping Gear

    Most of the time you're going to be hunting in remote high deserts. Cutting your hunting time by several hours every day so you can drive to and from your hotel, motel or B&B is a cost you will want to avoid. Tents, lanterns, water, food, all extend your time in the field.

## Licenses Required

None, but see Permission To Collect under "Foraging"

## Getting Started

Getting your feet wet in meteor hunting is pretty easy. You need a stick, a magnet, transportation, and sunblock. Like all the foraging professions, it's a good idea to test the waters before jumping in.

### Is this for me?

Because meteorites weather away over time, most meteor hunting is done in areas which have low rainfall. Because they're also a hobbyist hunting prize, the more accessible hunting areas are also the most picked over. This means that the best places to look for profitable fields are remote deserts. If you're not an outdoors person, this is definitely not the job for you.

Like most jobs in the Foraging category, the income is extremely variable because your gathering is extremely variable. It's possible to make a multi-day trip to a well-researched and proven area and return with nothing to show for it except for some very large expenses on your balance sheet. Thus, like most jobs in the Foraging category, patience is a very necessary quality in successful meteor hunters.

### Market Research

The market for meteorites is extremely "inefficient" from an economist's perspective: the commodity is a non-essential, demand is specialized and uneven, supply is unsteady, fakes are a concern, and the total size of the market is small. All this makes for an uncertain market, so having a large inventory is risky. That said, quality is usually the differentiator, and as a professional your pieces will generally be high quality, so you will have the best chance to get the highest prices available.

## Get Your Equipment

See the note about getting your feet wet. Don't blow a huge amount of money until you're sure you want to do this professionally.

## Target a search area

Sources for target areas abound. Google, meteor hunter Web sites, news reports of nighttime fireball sightings, etc., are all places you can start. There have even been meteor hunting tours, if you want the deluxe option. Later on, your own research will be your best guide to where you want to go for hunts.

## Get permission to collect

As with most of the foraging professions, you will need permission to collect goods off the land in question. This is always the case on private land, but may also be true even on public land. Always check before collecting. If it's private land, often a simple phone call is enough to garner permission. Later, when you may be gathering more valuable meteors, you may want to get a lawyer to draft a simple "lease to gather meteorites", and get the owner to sign it. A lease will save you a lot of time in court if you get a valuable find, and the landowner forgets they gave you permission.

## Collect your meteorites

Walk and flick your magnet at black surface rocks. Walk and use your metal detector to find subsurface meteors. Walk and use your eyes to find non-ferrous meteors. Walk and… you get the idea.

## Get Paid

The actual marketplace for meteors is (for the most part) person-to-person, it's somewhat like selling paintings, except there are far fewer professional galleries. There are specialized Web sites, plus eBay & craigslist and things like that. There are also private mailing lists and catalogs, and some auction houses (even Christie's) will sell appropriately valuable specimens and collections. A lot of the professional meteor hunter crowd seems to host their own Web site, complete with pictures and narratives of the individual meteors they have for sale.

## Getting Good

The number of professional meteor hunters worldwide is actually vanishingly small. This has its upsides and its downsides. The upside is that there's a lot of room to become the top dog. The downside is that there is no hard science about how to be the best, just a lot of guesswork and opinion. Experience and the contacts you make will be your best teachers.

## Other Resources

- United States Bureau of Land Management
- State Mineral Resources Board

# Animal Services

Americans love animals, and if you're an animal lover, this means plenty of job opportunities for you.

## The working environment

Fur, like time, flies. You'll be working with animals, which carries its own distinct risks and rewards. Scratches, bites, and the occasional bug bite are things you will have to live with or defend well against.

## The Pay

The pay for pet-related jobs is moderate. None of these jobs, even working at the highest tier, pay as much as the professional contracting jobs, for instance. That is not to say you can't make a living doing them. These are jobs you *want* to take and which bring satisfaction in addition to a livable wage.

## Conclusion

These jobs are not for everybody, but the people who like them, **love** them.

# 22
# Farrier

*Horse shoes.*

About 1400 years ago, someone in western Europe thought it might be a good idea to nail a horseshoe onto the horse's hoof, rather than trying to bind it on with leather. Ever since, fitting horseshoes and shoeing horses has been in demand.

**N.B.** Don't confuse "Farrier" with "Furrier", which is someone who trades animal skins, pelts, and fur.

## The Pay

The pay (for shoeing) is actually fairly low, but you'll charge a "per visit" fee as well as a "per hoof" fee, and that will make up the difference.

## Training

There actually *are* farrier schools, but they aren't required to do this work. Mostly you'll get on-the-job training working with a different farrier.

## Equipment

*Required*

- Horseshoes, Hammer, Nails, etc.
- Hoof Knife, File
- Chaps

*Good To Have*

- Spare everything, including clothing.

## Licenses Required

No state that I could find required a license to be a professional farrier *outside* the horse-racing field. Virtually *every* state with sanctioned horse racing requires farriers working on racehorses to be licensed.

## Getting Started

### Is this for me?

Despite the dreams of endless numbers of 12-year-old girls, horses (particularly work horses) are not always friendly giants with clean coats and good manners. They're not small, not easily managed, and can spoil your day (or month) with a kick or a step if you're not careful. Handling large animals is definitely not for everybody. Best to do a ride-along with another farrier before plunging in.

### Market Research

It may surprise you to learn that there are almost as many farriers on Manhattan Island as there are in any other city or town. A lot of cities have relatively extensive "horse property" neighborhoods, and they all need farriers, so this is not a rural-areas-only kind of job.

### Get Trained

You can learn how to shoe a horse in under an hour. It's not a complicated task, unless you need to remake the shoe. Getting to the point where both you *and* the animal are comfortable with the process takes practice. For your first several months, just focus on getting the job done right, and not how much you're making. Speed will come with practice.

### Do It!

After a couple of practice runs (or weeks of practice runs) with another farrier, you just have to try it on your own. If you need additional practice animals, check with the local veterinary college, and ask if you can work on their animals.

*Get Paid*

This is most often a cash business, although checks or credit cards will show up occasionally.

## Getting Good

As with most of the jobs in this section, getting good relies in large part on developing a good "hand" with animals, and that's something that comes with time and attitude.

More so than most dog owners, horse owners can be persnickety about your work. Don't be shocked if you're asked to redo something, or blamed for something that wasn't remotely your fault. Budget time for it, and up the bill. You're going home with their money, after all. Be nice about it.

## Other Resources

- American Farriers Association
- Brotherhood of Working Farriers
- World Farrier's Association

# 23

# Large Aquarium Maintenance

*Get paid to be coy!*

Large aquariums are a beautiful feature in a home, but require more maintenance than most homeowners want to put out. That's where you come in.

## The Pay

The pay is usually monthly, and is based on aquarium size, environment, and the number of visits you make per month. It's massively variable, but is well over $20 an hour, and ranges up to hundreds (or more) per month for complicated sites.

## Training

There are no large-scale schools on large aquarium maintenance that I could find, but there is a *lot* of informal information out there. There's a lot you can get wrong, and the information changes regularly, so you will definitely need to keep up with the industry whether you have a degree, certificate, or just experience.

## Equipment

*Required*

- Water analysis toolkit
- Fix-it box (pH, saline, antibiotic treatments, etc)
- Replacement air and water filters
- Glass (inner and outer) cleaning gear

*Good To Have*

- Replacement bulbs & heating elements

## Licenses Required

No municipality I could find has a licensing requirement for aquarium maintenance, although several specialty product manufacturers offer certificates in the application and use of their products.

## Getting Started

### Is this for me?

I know this sounds obvious, but if you don't like getting wet, or if touching snails, algae, sea cucumbers, or fish bothers you, this may not be the job for you.

This job also requires a lot of reading to keep up to date on the latest techniques and traps in the industry, so if business-related reading (or making time for it) is a challenge, you probably want to look for a different career path.

### Market Research

Market research is probably more important for this job than for almost any other in this book. Large aquariums are not added to houses every day, so your market is fairly static. If there aren't any customers within 20 miles, this may not be a viable job.

First steps are easy: talk to the local tropical fish stores and find out who has the really big aquariums in the area. Follow up with the luxury homebuilders (and contractors) in the area and find out if they've put any in recently. Lastly, customers putting in large aquariums often contact the local college's marine biology department to ask for advice. It's possible the professors can point you to people in need of your services.

### Get Trained

The first time you add the wrong kind of salt to an aquarium, and kill ten thousand dollars worth of rare fish, you're going to realize the value of training and education. That is, assuming you survive the process of informing the owner.

Unfortunately, with few or no schools offering "Large Aquarium Maintenance" degrees, a lot of your training will be self-taught, mostly by reading. There are a huge number of magazines, books, and Web sites devoted to large scale aquariums, and keeping up with the latest is going to be important.

One last thing: people *do* keep dangerous animals in their aquariums, so be careful. Predators and prey both have weapons, and a jellyfish sting, octopus bite, or fish spine can all send you to the hospital if they're from the wrong species. Being careful requires being informed. Be both.

## Do It!

The work itself is pretty straightforward, but requires some record keeping.

1.  Examine the aquarium visually

    What's the water like? Cloudy? Dark? What's the water level? What's the glass like? Clear? Scratched? Algified? Make notes of all of these.

2.  Check the instruments & logs if any

    Check the temp, salinity, oxygen gauges, if any. More importantly check (and copy) their logs, if they keep them. Make notes.

3.  Check the filters

    Air & Water. Likely there are multiples of each. Record their status

4.  Analyze the water

    What you look for is going to vary (a lot) from aquarium to aquarium. Salt or fresh, warm or cold, animals, plants, and coral will all matter what you test for an how often. Make notes.

5.  Fix any problems

    Clean the tank, replace the filters, adjust the temperature, oxygen level, etc. Adjust the water as needed. Doctor the fish as needed. Record all of this.

## Get Paid

This is usually on a periodic basis: monthly, quarterly, etc. They may pay you by check, or it's easy enough to set up a recurring credit card charge if you have the right clearinghouse. Keep in mind that the people who have these high-end aquariums are relatively affluent, and expect you to be both professional and flexible. Happily, they also pay well.

## Getting Good

Read. Read more. Go to conferences. Attend classes and in-services. Talk to other people in your industry. Stay on top of the news in your industry. Your customers don't just expect it, they will demand it.

Dealing with the affluent is a little different as well. Not in the yes-sir/no-sir way, but in the we're-both-good-at-what-we-do way. If there are doubts on either side, your business will suffer. Your greatest personal selling point is probably having a bunch of good references. Keeping your current customers satisfied will get you more.

Lastly remember that your image does matter here, like it does in all businesses where you enter someone else's home. Be neat, both personally and with your job. Smell good. Don't leave *any* trash around when you leave. Stuff like that. Taking an extra 5 whole minutes per job to make sure you've done the whole job, and cleaned up as well, will pay itself back in spades.

## Other Resources

If you *have* a large (visitor) aquarium in your city, by all means get to know the folks behind the scenes there. Likewise, if a local college has a marine biology department, it's a great place to meet other people who know what you want to learn. Check your yellow pages for a veterinarian that works on fish specifically. They'll have a load of good info.

Beyond that, the library is your best resource. Keep reading, every day, and your income will increase proportionally.

# 24
# Obedience Trainer

*Sit! Stay! Roll Over!*

Rover, Rex, and Princess all occasionally need their manners improved. That's where you come in.

## The Pay

Obedience training can be done one-on-one, or in groups, and can be done at a facility or your customer's home. Group rates, for four to eight weekly one-hour classes, run from $40 to $125. That works out to between $5 and $31 per hour per dog in the class.

Private lessons are substantially more ($40-$100/hr) but the owners usually demand assurances that the training works, and won't generally lay out that kind of money without references and referrals.

## Training

There's a lot of good information out there in books and videos. Some specialty fields (stunt pets, guard animals, etc) also have formal training available. For the most part, though, it's just read, practice, and see what works for you.

## Equipment

### Required

- A place to work

  If you're not restricting yourself to working only at your clients' homes, you'll need to find a place to work that's available on a regular basis. Many towns and cities have dog-friendly parks where you can get permission to teach. Many churches and schools will also make their grassy areas available to you if you promise to keep them clean.

*Good To Have*

- Spare leashes, water bowls, tugging ropes, and fetching objects

  Many, many times an owner will arrive short one of these things, and it's hard to get the dog focused if he's running around, too hot or too bored. Having spares is enormously useful.

- Treats/Rewards, food and otherwise

  Rewarding good behavior is something that everyone needs to do, and finding out that this particular dog doesn't like that particular variety of doggy snack (even when selected by the owner) can stop you in your tracks, so have some backups.

## Licenses Required

No state or municipality I could find required a license to be an Obedience Trainer.

## Getting Started

*Is this for me?*

If you're allergic to- or afraid of- dogs, this probably isn't the best job for you.

*Market Research*

Like other personal service jobs (such as Massage Therapist) the market is usually what you make of it. There may be dozens of dog trainers in your area, or none at all, but depending on the demand level and skill of the available trainers, either might be a great opportunity, or a hopeless cause.

Talk to your local pet store owners, particularly the smaller neighborhood ones. Find out who they're referring people to, and why. Ask if there are any niches that need filling. Your city or county "Parks and Recreation" organization may also have similar information. Do not base *any* decisions on the first couple of conversations… fan out and ask lots of people at lots of different stores. Get way too much data, then make your call.

### Get Trained

For the most part, there's no special training. You learn the basics from books, magazines, videos, etc., and practice practice practice.

### Do It!

Practice makes perfect. Work your skill.

### Get Paid

In almost all cases, you'll be paid immediately before or after the lesson, by check, cash, or sometimes credit card.

## Getting Good

This, as with many service jobs, is as much about how you please the owner as much as how well you did the job. Figuring out what the owner really wants (less barking) and getting it to them is more important than doing what they asked for in the first place. Get along with the dogs and the masters, keep them both happy, and you'll be a huge success.

## Other Resources

- National Association of Dog Obedience Trainers (NADOT)
- Association of Pet Dog Trainers (APDT)
- The ASPCA

# 25
## Traveling Pet Groomer

*Good grooming isn't just for people*

Spot, Puss-puss, and Precious all occasionally need their coats cleaned, claws trimmed, and skin scrubbed. Owners may solve this by making an appointment with the groomer, with the associated hassle of dropping off and picking up their pet on the groomer's schedule. Or for a premium price the owners can save themselves driving, headaches, and time by having you come to them,

## The Pay

An individual grooming session (for a pet, not a show dog) can run from $30 to $100. A session typically takes about an hour because there's a lot more than just whipping out the clippers and shearing off the spare fur. That, plus travel expenses, does put a limit on the amount of money you can make in a week, but it's quite possible to make a comfortable living.

## Training

There's a lot of good information out there in books and videos. There are even style magazines! For the most part, though, it's just read, practice, and see what works for you.

## Equipment

### Required

- A work area

  Most traveling groomers have a step-van where they can take care of all but the very largest animals.

- A selection of soaps

  You're going to run into a fair number of allergies and/or preferences on the part of the animals and their owners, and you've got to be ready to handle all of them. Have a wide selection of manufacturers and types

- Spare leashes, water bowls, and toys

  You can't do your job on an uncontrollable animal. Be prepared to cover anything the owner might've forgotten. They're paying a premium to avoid aggravation, and you don't want to add any.

- Treats/Rewards, food and otherwise

  Finding out that this particular dog doesn't like that particular variety of doggy snack can cause you trouble, so have some backups.

- Bows and Frippery

  Giving the pooch or puss that extra-cutesy touch goes a long, long way with many owners. Never forget that pleasing them is your first priority.

## Licenses Required

As far as I can tell, there are no required licenses. Most of the licenses in this area I could find dealt with boarding, rather than grooming. There are a large number of companies that offer certifications in various methods. When in doubt, contact your city hall.

## Getting Started

### Is this for me?

If you're allergic to- or afraid of- dogs, cats, horses, or other domestic and domesticated animals, this probably isn't the best job for you.

### Market Research

Just as with Animal Trainer, the market is usually what you make of it. Talk to your local kennel clubs and pet store owners. Find out who they're referring people to, and why. Ask if there are any needs unmet or niches that need filling. Don't base any decisions on the first couple of conversations. Get lots of data, then decide.

### Get Trained

For the most part, there's no special training. You learn the basics from books, magazines, videos, etc., and practice practice practice. Various companies offer certifications in various methods of grooming, but that is probably more a marketing than a skill consideration.

### Get Your Equipment

Like any job that suggests business transportation, the up-front cost can be considerable. Look around and see what other people are doing. Find out what works and what doesn't. It's no good to get an old Dodge Econo-van with a great grooming stand replacing the table if you're going to be working with horses and large breed dogs. This is definitely a case where a little preparation and planning can save you a lot of money.

### Do It!

Like many businesses, a grooming business starts slow, and grows with referrals and references. Do everything right, even when you only have one appointment a day, it's during rush traffic, it's miles away, and the owner is using a coupon. Eventually, doing it right will pay off.

### Get Paid

In almost all cases, you'll be paid immediately before or after the session, by check, cash, or sometimes credit card.

## Getting Good

Keeping the owners satisfied is *at least* as important as getting their dog completely clean. Make sure you're doing what the owner wants, not just what they asked for. Take the time to listen carefully to what they tell you: you'll earn a lot more in the long term from happy masters and clean-ish dogs than you will from semi-satisfied masters and completely clean dogs.

## Other Resources

- National Dog Groomer's Association of America (NDGAA)
- International Association of Canine Professionals (IACP)
- New England Pet Grooming Professionals

# 26
## Animal Caretaker
*Vacation Fill-in*

While we've all head of the job "pet sitter", it doesn't actually seem to be a real job anywhere I could find: it's usually easier for a family with a dog or cat (or both) to either board their pets or leave them with friends when they need time away.

That said, farmers, animal breeders, and kennel owners all take vacations too, and it's much harder to find a neighbor willing to look after 200 head of cattle than a well-trained Labrador. There is actually money to be made taking care of larger facilities like farms.

## The Pay

The pay is highly variable, but easily outstrips minimum wage, even at the lower end. This is, as they say, "real work", and you'll get paid reasonably well for doing it.

## Training

Experience is important, so you may need to volunteer some time at first, to learn how to handle various types of animals. Taking care of a kennel full of puppies and taking care of a herd of cattle require completely different skill sets. In this job, you'll be doing both, so getting hands-on experience with every local animal business is useful.

## Equipment

This is highly specific to the kinds of animals you're dealing with, but frequently you'll be caring for them while they're on the owner's premises, so it's likely a lot of the specialty gear will already be there for you.

## Licenses Required

You may indeed need an animal handling license, depending on your area. Contact the county Department of Agriculture and find out what's required.

## Getting Started

### Is this for me?

Obviously, this is (for the most part) outside work. It's also "dirty". If you're a bookish sort, this may not be the job for you. Another important consideration is handling surprises. You'll be operating independently, and handling "whatever comes up", which can include sick animals, or lost animals, or power outages, or… well… lots of things. If you're not comfortable thinking on your feet and using your judgment (and then later defending your decisions) then you probably want a different job.

### Market Research

For the most part, this job does not exist in urban environments. If you live in a very urban environment, don't be surprised to find no one in need of your services.

That said, your county department of agriculture is a great place to start. They'll have a complete tally of all the local animal businesses, as well as a schedule of free "farm walks" you can go on to see how the local businesses do their business. Make friends with your DepAg people. They will be very important to your success.

### Get Trained

Volunteer at farms and breeding businesses. Attend every Farm Walk you can manage. Go to county fairs and ask questions. There *are* schools which offer 2- and 4- year programs in animal husbandry and animal care, and people with a degree will command more money, but even without a formal degree you can get work, if you have experience and references.

### Do It!

It goes without saying that whoever is leaving their animals in your hands is going to be a Nervous Nellie the first few times they work with you. Expect a lot of check-up phone calls and a lot of their friends & neighbors "just stopping by" to check on you. When you have a long-term independent job like this, it's essential you do it *right*. Get caught hosting a party, or playing wrong with the animals, feeding them late, or missing a "down" animal just once, and you're never getting work from this guy (or the other farmers around here) again. This is one of those "keep your nose clean" jobs- don't forget it.

### Get Paid

You'll get paid when the job is done. Sometimes there's an "everything went perfectly" bonus, but most of the time it's a flat fee. Most often it will be cash or check. Rarely will you handle a credit card.

## Getting Good

Breadth of experience means a lot, being able to handle whatever animals are in need of care is a big deal. Depth of experience is too. This is definitely a reference-based business. Your reputation is going to count for a lot. Defend it by doing your job right every time.

Having good contacts with the local veterinarians, department of agriculture, and other local farmers is a big deal, since calling them is a "less big deal" than calling the owner, who is, after all, trying to relax on vacation. If you can solve the problem without them, they'll be much more comfortable leaving their animals with you in the future.

## Other Resources

- County Department of Agriculture
- 4H, FFA, AKC, and similar organizations
- Local colleges' schools of agriculture

# TEACHING AND COACHING

There are a lot of people out there who are either trying to learn something new, or get better at something they can already do. Sometimes it's for their work, and other times it's just for fun.

There is little glamor for tutors, teachers and coaches, but the people they help remember them forever. Everyone has a story about a favorite mentor of one type or another who helped them get to the next level. You can be that person for someone else, even if you don't (yet) know what you want to teach.

This section of the book describes four jobs (Music Teacher, Language Teacher, Personal Fitness Trainer, and Dance Instructor) which devote themselves to helping other people get better at a skill.

## Is there work?

The simple answer is yes. There is always demand for teaching and coaching. In this regard these jobs are exactly like the ones in the professional contracting section: there is *always* room at the top. If you ask around among people who are taking classes themselves or are sending their kids, you can always find a bunch saying "Oh my gosh! We drive all the way out to [...] for lessons because we can't find anyone nearer!" That's a sure sign there's room in your area.

## A word of warning

People who are naturally skilled at these things are often the worst teachers & coaches. People who make good music teachers are people who can spend days on end listening to good music played very badly, and take pleasure in the small improvements over time. Someone who is a great pianist might not be able to stand that environment for ten minutes. Likewise, anything that comes naturally to someone is very hard for that person to explain to someone else. The best teachers and the best practitioners are often very different people.

## 27
# Music Teacher

*Music to the ears - someday*

The old stereotype is parents forcing their kids to take piano or violin lessons. In reality there are a lot of people, young and old, who really do want to learn to play.

## The Pay

Music teachers make $20-$100/hr for one-on-one sessions. While that is quite a spread, top-tier specialists can make even more. Since people sign up for sets of lessons lasting several months, the pay is quite steady as well.

## Training

Somewhat surprisingly, no one expects a piano teacher to be a virtuoso. (see the "Mentoring" section note) The training you need is often more about music theory and working with people. There are not a lot of schools who teach music education, although there are a few. Mostly you need to build up some area knowledge, get a few happy clients, and work from referrals.

## Equipment

This depends a lot on where you're teaching. If you're teaching piano, and teaching at your home, you'll need a piano. Otherwise, students will generally bring their own instruments to the session, whether you're holding it at your home, theirs, or a local music store's practice room

## Licenses Required

I could find *no* municipality where there was any kind of required licensing to teach music. While certificates look nice hanging on the wall, your references are far more likely to impress your students.

# Getting Started

## *Is this for me?*

Teaching music is about enjoying the student's improvement, *not* their music. Part of teaching is continually encouraging the student to try things they're not good at (*yet*), so 90% of the music you ever hear your student play will contain wrong notes and bad meter. If that's going to set your teeth on edge, this may not be the job for you.

## *Market Research*

The hands-down best place to find information about local music teachers is at the local music stores and high schools. The owners and teachers will be sure to know everyone within a fair distance who's been known to teach a given instrument, and can often offer gossip about what people are looking for now.

## *Get Trained*

This is both easy and hard. Taking some local extension classes on working with and teaching kids (or adults) is going to help. If you've been a music student at one point or another, that'll help too. But since most of your business will come from your references rather than your certificates, getting trained is a pretty quick process.

## *Prepare*

You *will* need a series of lesson plans. You *will* need to "slot" your students into them, and you *will* need to track their progress carefully, so do your preperatory work ahead of each lesson.

There are mountains of freely available lesson plans for music teachers online. Find ten you like, download and read them all, and choose one your student likes.

Keep records of progress. Some people (whether the students are adults or children) will actually want a sort of "report card" from time to time, and if you have no records, you're stuck.

*Do It!*

Once you've actually got your students sitting (or standing) in front of you, a lot of the "work" is managing the student through the lesson plan. Be patient, and listen to the student, not their music. If they're confused, try changing lesson plans, putting things in a different order, or rephrasing things. They can't improve if they can't see the way forward.

*Get Paid*

Sometimes you will be paid session-by-session, usually by cash or check. Just as often, though, you'll be paid for a group of lessons, monthly, or on some other regular basis. In these cases payment will almost always be by check.

## Getting Good

A good teacher is pretty much defined as one who's helping students improve rapidly. Improvement during one-on-one teaching has a lot to do with the teacher-student relationship, and just like everywhere else, some people get along and others don't. One aspect of getting good is "knowing when to say when" and helping a struggling student find a different teacher.

The best way to shine in this field is via your reputation. What people are saying about you when you're not in the room is your most valuable asset, so a certain amount of "getting good" is also strictly social. Getting along with the students (and parents, if any) will take you a long way.

Beyond that, "good" usually means you have the widest possible reach: lots of teaching styles, lots of lesson plans, lots of different approaches. The more people you can actually work with and improve, the better off you'll be.

## Other Resources

- Music Teachers National Association (MTNA)
- The National Association for Music Education (MENC)
- Several states (including California, Michigan, and Texas) have their own Music Teacher associations

# 28
# Language Teacher

*Hablo, Parle, Spreche, ad infinitum*

There are far many subcategories of language teacher. Local people hire language teachers to learn a foreign language, immigrants hire language teachers to learn the local language. Both might hire a dialect coaches to improve (or eliminate) their accent, and there are other variations as well. This chapter will focus this section on one-on-one teaching for a second language, assuming the teacher and student share fluency in a first common language.

## The Pay

Language teachers earn $20-$100/hr for one-on-one lessons. Dialect coaches are slightly higher at both ends, since they have to have top-tier native fluency in the target language.

## Training

There are a lot of places that will help *you* learn a second language, but similar to most of the jobs in this section, not a lot of places that will teach you how to teach. Training is pretty much an on-the-job situation.

That said, there are certain students (government employees, for instance) that may want certain kinds of certifications when they finish your class. Some of these certificates may require you to be certified in some particular system. Others may require your students to pass a standardized test. If you want to teach *these* students (and that's certainly not mandatory) you might need to do some additional work first.

## Equipment

### Required

- A textbook
- Samples of native speakers speaking

*Good To Have*

- A recorder so the student can hear their own voice
- Lots of sources (online, textual, audio) for additional vocabulary for your students.

## Licenses Required

I could not find any municipality where there was a licensing requirement for teaching languages.

## Getting Started

*Is this for me?*

Two characteristics, patience and attention to detail, are absolute requirements for this job. If you're someone who needs a lot of stimulation to keep your mind on work, this is definitely not the job for you. Almost every time your student speaks, you'll know what they *mean* to say. If your brain glosses over the wrong verb, wrong tense (or even wrong language) after you've been listening for half an hour, then you're doing a bad job for your student.

*Market Research*

Good places to do your market research are schools. Find out who the school's teachers recommend, and ask what they would like to see but can't find.

*Prepare*

Like all the jobs in this section, lesson plans and progress tracking are an absolute must. There are a million sources online for lesson plans, and a million more available at your local schools.

You have a lot of control over your success with a given student if you spend the time prepping properly.

Breadth of teaching techniques and material is the same thing as cash in the bank. Don't stick with one way to explain how to pronounce "Xingyiquan", have five. Recognize that students have individual accents and patterns of speech, so saying than "ten" rhymes with "pen" may not help if they have a northeast urban accent, so "pin" and "pen" are pronounced identically.

Keeping notes on a per-student basis will really pay off here, and certainly make learning easier for the student.

## Do It!

Once you've got your student or students, managing the student through the lesson plan is your primary goal. Be equal parts encouraging and honest. They're paying you for your patience as much as their progress. Keep that in mind, and don't let yourself get frustrated.

## Get Paid

Like most of the jobs in this section, you may be paid session-by-session, usually by cash or check. Just as often, though, you'll be paid for a group of lessons, monthly, or on some other regular basis. In these cases payment will almost always be by check.

# Getting Good

Good teachers are teachers whose students make progress. Progress for your students will depend (to a certain degree) on how you both get along. If a particular student isn't getting what they're paying for because the two of you aren't a "good match", recommend them to another teacher. Your reputation will increase and the student will shine, and that will make up for the short-term loss of income.

Keep in mind that your patience and their progress are the two things they want- and they're paying the bills.

# Other Resources

Foreign-Language resources

- American Council on the Teaching of Foreign Languages
- Several states (including Indiana and Arkansas) have local Foreign Language Teachers Associations.

Accent-related Resources

- American Speech–Language–Hearing Association (ASHA)
- Voice & Speech Trainers Association (VASTA)
- Accent Reduction Training Academy (ARTA)

# 29
# Personal Fitness Trainer

*Everyone wants to look better in the mirror*

The tagline for 24 hour fitness is rumored to be *"Look better naked!"* None of us want to think that way, but to some extent, all of us do.

In the United States the fitness industry is huge. Lots of people sign up for gym memberships, buy treadmills, track suits, and running shoes, and then let them all collect dust. Things rarely motivate people.

There are a variety of categories of fitness trainer, but for the purposes of this article, we're going to focus on independent trainers (not affiliated with a particular location or franchise) who do one-on-one training with their customers, whether at the customer's home or a facility the trainer uses.

## The Pay

Personal Fitness Trainers charge between $20 and $200 an hour, depending on their credentials and the intensity of the workload the customer wants. The pay is a little less steady than some of the other jobs in this section, because many things can happen that will sideline a fitness program that would not necessarily get in the way of a language lesson.

## Training

There are a huge number of facilities out there that will train (and certify) you as a personal trainer. Being good at any general training regimen is sufficient to start. You don't need the latest buzzwords to be successful in the short or long term.

Interestingly, most people who have been active personal trainers for more than five years at a stretch don't actually have any of the "new, cool" certificates. Most of them don't even hang their old ones. Fitness training (fitness in general) is no more "new" than the human body, and that's been around in its current form for thousands of years.

## Equipment

Whether you're meeting at the customer's home (and using his equipment) or at a facility of your choice (and using their equipment) there isn't much you really need to have yourself.

## Licenses Required

Assuming you're not doing medical or rehabilitation work, there are generally no licenses required to be a personal fitness trainer. For physical therapy, professional sports training, etc., you may need a certificate or license. That's a separate path though, and not one we're dealing with here.

## Getting Started

### Is this for me?

Like a massage therapist, you're going to be in a fair amount of direct physical contact with your clients: spotting, adjusting grips and stance, etc. If you're uncomfortable being around people of different races, genders, or body shapes, this may not be a good choice for you. Likewise, if you are personally physically weak or accident prone, you might actually be a hazard to your students in some of these cases. Be honest with yourself about whether this is something you can really do.

### Market Research

Well, here's the bad news: these days it seems like one person in every ten US citizens is a personal fitness trainer with some organization or another. (Another one in ten is a martial arts instructor of some kind, but that's a different story)

There's really nothing for it but to jump in and try. Work from your recommendations, referrals, and references.

### Get Trained

Particularly when you first want to get started, being associated with a particular program can be useful. It will bring you into contact with the customer base, and also give you an idea of what you have to look forward to. A lot of personal fitness trainers start with one franchise or trade-name, and it can be a good way to start.

Others stay independent their whole careers. For them, their training is strictly on-the-job. Both can work very well

## Do It!

Once your student is in front of you, the two things you want to keep in mind are: patience and progress. Your student is paying you for both, even when they're six foot six, two eighty, and say they're looking for a tough-as-nails bootcamp program.

A word to the wise: Your students will be less interested than you are in physical training. If they were as interested as you are, they'd be personal trainers too, instead of doing what they do. Remember that your student is paying your bills. Keep any frustration you might feel about their commitment or their progress to yourself. It's their money, they can spend it how they like.

## Get Paid

There *are* personal trainers who get paid retainers, or on a monthly basis, but the vast majority are paid by-the-session in cash or check. Being able to take credit cards may be a plus, but it's definitely not mandatory.

## Getting Good

Progress and Patience. If the student has the first and you have the second, then congratulations, you're doing well.

Beyond that, getting broader exposure to more kinds of training and more methods of motivating your students is going to broaden your potential customer base, decrease your stress level, and increase your income. Expand both.

## Other Resources

There are a million associations specializing in this area. Two examples are:

- International Sports & Fitness Trainers Association
- National Association for Fitness
- National exercise Trainers Association

And don't ignore the federal government:

- American Heart Association

# 30
# Dance Instructor

*Lead or follow!*

There more ways to dance than there are people on earth, but dancing, and "dancing well enough to feel comfortable doing it in public" are two different things. That's where you come in.

## The Pay

The pay, like most instruction jobs, is quite reasonable: $20-$80/hr is doable immediately, with more money available for specialized or higher level instruction.

## Training

Unlike a lot of jobs in this section, there are quite a few schools to teach people who want to teach dance. Most large-franchise dance studios offer instruction for instructors, and this can be genuinely valuable. Talk to other people in the field (visit a few studios) and ask around to see where they learned their craft.

## Equipment

## Required

- Dance Shoes

  Unlike some teaching jobs, you *will* be expected to be able to do what you're teaching. Every day. So comfortable dance-wear, particularly including shoes, is important.

- Music

  You will be expected to provide the music as well, so whether it's a boom box, stereo, or iPod Nano with an amplifier, you need to bring the notes to the students.

## Good To Have

- Video play gear with slow motion/stop

  No matter *how* good you are, you won't physically be able to do demonstrate everything your student might want to try, so having a collection of dance video and playback gear will save you some physical strain.

## Licenses Required

Like most jobs in this category, I could find no place that required a license to teach dance. But certificates from various authorities (Arthur Murray, etc) may be of use when attracting clients.

## Getting Started

### Is this for me?

You're going to be in direct physical contact with your customer base, so if touching people of a specific gender, race, or form is difficult for you, this may not be a good job choice.

### Market Research

Every city and most towns host a dance studio or two. Visit them and find out what the market is like. Do people want individual instruction at their house, or group instruction at a facility? Do they want Ballroom, Modern, Street, Tap or what? Who's teaching? What's not being taught?

### Prepare

Like the other teaching jobs, having a broad repertoire will be helpful. Don't bring 2 videos, bring 20. Don't bring one CD of music, bring 50. Don't show *one* variation of the foxtrot, show a dozen. Tracking student progress is important as well. Keep notes- your income will grow.

### Do It!

Part of this work is going to be balancing your own self consciousness with your desire to let it all hang out. Too far to either extreme will make your instruction less attractive. To the greatest degree possible, get your students involved in the demonstration phase. What they show you will be at least as helpful as what they ask for when it comes to your lesson plans.

## Get Paid

Whether in a studio or private setting, most students will pay for a "term" of some number of lessons (4, 6, 8, etc) all at once, and almost always up-front. Like music instruction, refunds are usually heavily qualified. You may get paid in cash, credit card, or check, so be flexible enough to handle all three easily.

# Getting Good

Keep a close eye on your students. They may be unwilling to say "That looks lame" or "I don't want to do *that* kind of thing", so the only direct feedback you're likely to get is that they don't come back next week. If you're getting a lot of one-and-done customers, spend more time watching their faces than their feet, and consider shifting to a different kind/format/step of dance.

Unlike some other "touch" professions (Massage, for instance) your customers may or may not be comfortable with the idea of you touching them directly. It's strange, but it's true. Some people (perhaps you included) are just naturally good at putting people at their ease, and this won't cause a problem.

But if you're not in the "naturally gifted" category, there is help to be had. Believe it or not there are actually workshops that people like chiropractors and dance instructors take to learn how to touch people without causing them stress. Attending one may be money well spent.

# Other Resources

- Professional Dance Instructors Association
- National Dance Teachers Association
- Some cities (including San Diego and Omaha) have their own dance instruction associations.

# RESIDENTIAL SERVICES

Given today's busy schedules, a lot of people are looking to get work done for themselves while they're doing their own job. These are jobs which get scheduled while they are not home.

# 31
# Pool & Spa Maintenance

*Oh pool boy...*

Today's higher end pools can require physical management of their equipment as well as just cleaning. Being the local business who offers the whole package will keep you ahead of the rest.

## The Pay

In the last two years, pay for pool maintenance has dropped a bit, due to an unusual change in the industry. Banks now have larger inventories of houses that they own, and thus that they need to care for. Pool maintenance is required in a lot of municipalities, so banks *used* to be a huge consumer of pool cleaning services. However, with the very large number of houses that banks are carrying, several of the larger banks have actually opened their own pool & property maintenance divisions, driving demand back down.

Even so, monthly rates for simple pool cleaning run $20 to $100, depending on the size and number of visits per month. Additionally, water features like Jacuzzis and coy ponds also need regular maintenance, including filters, pumps, heaters, etc. If you're someone who can handle all the maintenance, rather than just the cleaning, you'll command the higher income.

## Training

There is no trade school (really) for pool cleaning, although there are some places that offer classes. There *are* certificates to be had from various equipment manufacturers, though, and that will matter when trying to get the extra "maintenance" part of your contract, so keep up to date on both what's at your customer's facilities *and* the equipment that's new to the market.

## Equipment

### Required

- Skimming nets, hoses, pumps
- Water analysis equipment

### Good To Have

- Sunblock & Bug spray. This is an outdoor job.
- Backup water treatment & chemicals
- Dedicated transportation. One spill of chlorinating agent in your family minivan will set you back.

## Licenses Required

I could not find any municipality requiring licensing to be a pool cleaner, but there are always exceptions. Check with your city hall if you're wondering.

## Getting Started

### Is this for me?

This is definitely an outdoor job, so if you sunburn easily, are allergic to bee stings, have terrible allergies, or something similar, you will need to take precautions.

It's physical, but only mildly so. Toting the occasional 5 gallon tub of pool chlorine is about the hardest thing you'll do. That said, doing this from a wheelchair would probably be difficult.

### Market Research

Don't be dismayed if you see 300 entries in your local phone book under the heading "pool cleaning service". Like the professional contracting jobs, there's always room at the top for more. Ask around in the neighborhoods that have pools: who do they use? What do they like? What do they wish they had?

### Do It!

Show up on time. Wear clean clothes. Have your gear ready. Get the job done and be *ready* to leave on time. *Then* go and ask if they have any questions, or want anything else done. If no, you're done, and you'll leave a good impression. If so, and if you can do it without making you late for your next appointment, do it.

## Get Paid

Like most residential services, you'll be paid on a regular basis (usually monthly) and usually by check. But flexibility in handling cash or credit cards will make the occasional exception easier.

# Getting Good

It's definitely a service job, so your customer's opinion of how you did your job is very close to as important to how well you did it. Neat, tidy, polite, and making yourself understood (no heavy accent) are all in the "plus" category, and references are going to be very valuable when it comes to getting new customers.

There's a lot of money to be made doing small pool repairs as well. If you can replace tile (well) or repair cracks in concrete (well) or repaint outdoor flooring (well) then there's a lot of upside in side-jobs. Customers would rather not deal with *yet another* repair-person if they don't have to.

# Other Resources

- American Spa And Pool Pros (ASAPP)
- Independent Pool and Spa Service Association

# 32
# Mobile Car Detailing

*Shiny happy cars*

A lot of people, given the chance, would rather *not* spend the time to take their car in to be detailed. This is where a mobile car detailer comes in. While they're at work, you drive to their workplace and detail their car for them, saving them time, and earning you money.

## The Pay

The pay is actually pretty generous, especially if you can group multiple customers at the same building. A simple wash is $25 and up. Detailing is $100 and up.

## Equipment

Here's the catch. The equipment isn't cheap: it can run from hundreds of dollars for a portable water tank & sprayer into the mid thousands of dollars for a purpose-built towed detailing rig. You get what you pay for: easier and faster to use, more professional, longer lasting. Happily, you can start at one end and build up to the other.

## Required

- Portable water. It's unlikely the local business park will let you use their hose. A large tank (with heater, if possible) is a requirement.
- Soaps, brushes, sponges, towels, shammys
- A vacuum cleaner

### Good To Have

- LOTS of water
- Air fresheners
- vinyl & leather treatments

- Clean, Dry clothes for meeting with the customer

No municipality I could find requires a license to wash cars. Some states (California for instance) may have water runoff regulations that you should know about.

# Getting Started

## Is this for me?

This is an outdoor job, for the most part. You'll be getting wet, scrunching into small cars and reaching far under seats for loose soda cans. If being outdoors, wet, or touching someone else's food wrappers is going to send you into a screaming fit, then this is probably not the job for you.

## Market Research

In this particular business, unless you are in a big city like New York or Chicago, you will need to do your market research up front. That's no big deal. A dozen phone calls and/or visits will get you there.

While with *most* jobs it's safe to say "there's always room at the top", with the grouping discounts and relatively low barrier to starting a detailing business, this market can definitely get crowded. Ask around at the local drive-up detailers about who is working the mobile market. Ask at gated communities (because the detailers will be "on the list" to enter) and large office parks if they have regular detailing services.

## Get Trained

If you buy a specialty rig, then there's probably an "Instructional DVD" that came with it. Don't skip that. It'll be important later.

Other than that, there are some pretty good videos on youtube about "how to detail a car". Check them out. You can also buy videos and books about car detailing from sources like Amazon.com.

## Get Your Equipment

If you have the money to jump in at the higher end, that's probably the easier path. There are purpose-built mobile detailing rigs designed to be towed behind a car or truck. There are also step-vans that have been modified to be detailing vehicles in and of themselves. These are good choices if you can swing the expense, particularly if you can find them used but in good condition.

Otherwise, you may need to beef up your suspension and steering pumps: driving around with hundreds of gallons of water in your street vehicle is very different from your typical trip to the store.

### Do it!

This may seem obvious, but: do a *good* job. Your customers pay a premium to have their car detailed while they're at work, and they are expecting top-notch service. Doing a half-baked job just once can cost you all the customers you've built up at that location

### Get Paid

This is almost exclusively by credit card. You usually get the number over the phone when you take the call. Sometimes you'll get cash or a check, but credit cards are likely to be the most popular payment method.

## Getting Good

Market, market, market. Word-of-mouth is going to propagate more slowly at work, since people usually have their minds on business. A lot of your new clients will be walk-ups while you're doing someone else's car.

To really turbo charge your business, have fliers made up. Do *not* put them on windshields. The same people that care about how their car looks enough to get it a mobile detailing job *hate* to find fliers stuck to their car. One business I know regularly distributes their fliers to the restrooms of local business parks. Keep an eye out for bulletin boards too. The more customers you nail down for each location, the more time you spend detailing and not driving.

Beyond that, making life easy on your customer is the key. Simple things like calling customers on a monthly basis to see if they want another detail, asking them "same credit card as last time" rather than making them read it out again, that sort of thing. If you're easy to do business with, you'll get more business.

## Other Resources

- Auto Detailing Network
- International Detailing Association

# 33

## Exterminator

*Think Ghostbusters, but smaller-scale*

This is the job that people must have done while they're not at home: an exterminator visit. Every dwelling, large or small, rich or poor, has its share of bugs. Every owner wants them dead. That's where you come in.

## The Pay

The pay is pretty good. Usually your service will come with a three-month "job well done" guarantee, where once they've paid for the initial visit, any additional visits (because the bugs are back) are free. A visit starts at about $100, and scales up with square footage, both indoor and outdoor. A visit can take a couple (or a few) hours, so the per-hour is pretty good.

## Equipment

This varies a lot, depending on your methods, the bugs you're after, and the kinds of insecticides you use. Termites are usually "fended off" by little turrets buried in the yard. Fleas are often killed by fumigation (setting up a "bug bomb") and spiders are often handled with hand-spraying corners and cracks. "Green" insecticides require different dispersion gear, and the list goes on. Be prepared to need one of everything.

While it's not usually under the list of "Equipment", insurance is pretty much required for this job. No matter how careful you are, you will make the occasional mistake, and having insurance to cover you in these cases (especially when you're dealing with chemicals) is absolutely necessary. Don't start this business without liability insurance.

## Licenses Required

Virtually *every* state and municipality requires exterminators to be licensed. You're working with (and occasionally storing) poisonous chemicals. The city, police, and fire department want to know up-front what to expect if they have to deal with your home or vehicle. Talk to the staff at your city hall and ask them what you need to do.

## Getting Started

### Is this for me?

This business is all about bugs. If bugs are a problem for you, this is probably not a good career choice. Likewise, you'll be in people's houses, on their turf so to speak, so there will be dogs, kids, and messes when you visit. If you have a low tolerance for other families' living conditions, this may not be the job for you. Lastly, you're dealing with chemicals, and attention to detail is going to be very very important. Mixing the wrong stuff can cause all kinds of problems, so if you have severe ADHD or something similar, you should stay clear of exterminating.

### Market Research

Although most of the time you will be working for a single customer at a single residence, you will occasionally pick up a contract with an apartment, house flipper, or business park. For the most part you'll be marketing directly to residential neighborhoods, so it pays to find out who else is exterminating in your neighborhood.

On the subject of marketing to neighborhoods: One famous exterminating company in Southern California uses white pickup trucks with a giant (two feet in diameter) 3D model of a black widow spider on the door next to their name. Now *that* is marketing. Everyone knows what they do, and it keeps their brand name on everyone's mind.

### Get Trained

Like the other "strongly licensed" jobs in this book, you will need some sort of formal training using the gear, and the chemicals, you intend to use. There are many insecticide companies out there, and a lot of them provide (or refer) training in the use of their products. There may also be municipal or state classes you need to take for licensing. Be prepared.

All told, this is going to take *at least* two full-time workweeks. Figure 60+ hours of field training and at least 10 hours of classwork.

*Exterminate!*

There are no two ways about it: this is a serious job.

1. Have a checklist for things to look for before you start (pets, gas stoves, etc) and walk the whole property looking for trouble

2. Have a plan for how you'll handle each particular location: Don't spray yourself into a corner with no way to get back to a room that hasn't been treated yet. A plan *also* helps you make sure you can finish the job on time, so the owners can come back to a chemically safe home.

3. Double- and Triple- check your chemicals before starting. People and pets have allergies. Plants are intolerant of certain treatments. Certain fabrics require pretreatment or covering with drop-cloths, etc. Never forget you're dealing with poison.

4. Run the property again (when it's safe) to make sure the work got done right.

5. (optionally) Call the owner on your cellphone and remind them when it will be safe to enter the home. It never hurts to be clear.

*Get Paid*

You will usually get paid just before or just after you do the job. While you will most often be paid with a check or a credit card, you may also get cash from time to time. Be flexible.

## Getting Good

Things like the after-extermination phone call, and follow-up calls to make sure everything was done right are good ways to make sure your customer is happy. If they are, they're more likely to recommend you to their friends.

Likewise, ask if you can call back in 3 (or 6, or 12) months to see if they want another service. That can be a good way to keep business you already have: when the other exterminator comes knocking, the job is already done.

Have a wide variety of methods and insecticides: ones that work around plants, animals, fabrics, ones that avoid inflaming allergies, that sort of thing. The more variety you offer, the more likely you can help whatever customer that calls you.

A little woodworking/carpentry skill can be very helpful when dealing with termite infestations, since the customer's first question is going to be about whether they need to replace anything. Learning a little extra will get you known as a true professional.

## Other Resources

- National Pest Management Association
- California Structural Pest Control Board (It's representative of the more well-regulated states, and may answer some general questions)

# 34
# Dog Walker

*Master works late, and rover needs a walk*

Lots of people get a pet, and then have a life change that makes it harder for them to take care of it. A divorce, move, promotion, or sick relative can all suck up time that was once available to play with Rex. That's where you come in.

## The Pay

Dog walkers usually get *something* like $1/minute for walks. A 15 or 20 minute walk costs about $15 or $20. Simple.

## Equipment

### Required

- Clean-up bags.

Yes, you heard me. No leaving the waste behind. You're an adult. You can handle it. At least as far as the nearest outdoor trash can.

- Spare leashes. There is a brand of leash out there that comes in a kind of plastic-handled spool, and uses a woven nylon tape as a lead. These are well regarded by dog walkers and vets I talked to.

### Good To Have

- A good map of the area. No sense in you being bored to death by the same scenery every day. Find a new place to go.
- A clean pair of shoes. Walking in parks you may step in mud or other muck. Don't track it into your customer's home *or* your car. Have a spare set of shoes.

- Mace, or other dog repellent. If you get "charged" by an unfriendly dog, you'll need to be able to protect yourself and your furry ward.

## Licenses Required

So long as you are not boarding the animals overnight, I could not find any municipality that required a license to walk dogs.

## Getting Started

### Is This For Me

If you are afraid of dogs... Oh never mind, that's obvious. This is an outdoor job with all of the things that go with it. It's also an animal job, so the occasional scratch, nip, or bug bite will doubtless occur. Most people pretty much "know" whether a dog walking job is for them. Go with your gut.

### Market Research

There's always room at the top, so have no fear. This is a largely social job, and beyond your regular marketing efforts, you get a lot of business by one customer recommending you to another. People aren't particularly loyal to their existing walker, so if you show up, have a good attitude, a clean outfit and reasonable prices, you're likely to get a "trial" run. After that it's up to you.

### Do It!

This is a great opportunity to do several things at once: earn money, get exercise, play with dogs, and get the dogs some exercise as well. Oh, yeah, that last part is what you're being paid for. The other stuff is "for free".

### Get Paid

If you're being paid for each "walk" and there's someone home, chances are you'll get cash or a check each time you visit. If you're doing "terms" like "every Friday this month" then you are more likely to get a check at the beginning or end of the period. Credit cards are pretty rare.

## Getting Good

If you have two or more customers that live in the same neighborhood and their dogs get along, you can take them out together for a much better playtime than they'd get just walking up and down the greenbelt.

Keeping an eye out for other stuff, like when the dog might need a trip to the groomer, or noticing that the dog isn't feeling that well also makes a good impression. If no one's home, you can leave a note tied to his collar, or send an e-mail after you drop him off.

## Additional Resources

There isn't much that deals exclusively with dog walking, but the Association of Pet Dog Trainers (APDT) does have some.

# 35

# Handyman

*Everyone needs a helping hand, sometimes*

Nowadays a handyman is less about fixing a leaky faucet than it is helping move a chest of drawers or helping mount a flat-screen TV on the wall. Lots of people find it hard to ask friends or family for help with stuff like this, or would just rather pay someone to "do it right" the first time.

## The Pay

The pay is pretty good, starting at $30 an hour and going up from there. often there's a higher per-visit charge that includes the first hour, or something like that. It's really between you and your customers.

## Equipment

*Required*

- Duct Tape: it's cliché, but it can solve a myriad of problems.
- Tools of all kinds, from hammers to paintbrushes
- Glue, epoxy, grout, etc.

*Good To Have*

If you can find it at a hardware store, sooner or later you'll probably want it. Conduit bender? Check. Electrical Socket Polarity Checker? You betcha. Having one of everything isn't really an option unless you're a millionaire, but the closer you are, the more work you'll get.

## Licenses Required

Under the heading "handyman" you probably won't need a contractor's license or anything like that, because you're not going to be doing a lot of work independent of the owner's supervision. If it's an older woman who just wants her potted plants brought indoors, she'll be there. Likewise the guy who's getting his TV mounted. The customer technically supervises everything.

## Getting Started

### *Is this for me?*

Frustratingly, with work like this, you have no objective criteria for "a job done well". Basically you're there until time runs out or the customer is satisfied. If working on a loose definition of success is not your thing, this is definitely not the job for you.

Likewise, there's a lot of personal interaction here too. If you prefer to work alone or in a controlled environment, this is not a good career choice.

### *Market Research*

This is a largely word-of-mouth business, although getting an add in the yellow pages and sending out fliers is a must at first. It's also very hard to find out whether there's a lot of competition or not. You're probably going to have to jump in and try.

### *Do It!*

Remember: The job isn't done right until the customer says it is. They are the boss, you're the help. Keep that in mind, even when they try to do it all wrong. If you have a suggestion, make sure it's a polite one. If they don't take it, that's their call. That's the difference between a general contractor and a handyman. They're in charge, so the risk is theirs.

### *Get Paid*

Normally you'll be paid in cash or check at the end of your visit. Sometimes people will give you a credit card up front when they call. Being flexible helps.

## Getting Good

This is more of a "people" business than you might expect. The people who really excel at it seem to have a knack for getting along with the customer. Focus on that, and you'll get a lot of repeat business.

Know when to suggest that they hire a professional. If someone calls you for "an electrical problem" but wants to rewire their house and garden, it's time to throw in the towel and suggest a good electrician. You may not make money on *this* visit, but your customer will call you again when they need you.

## Other Resources

- Association of Certified Handyman Professionals (ACHP)
- Handyman Club of America (HCA)

# OTHER BUSINESS IDEAS

This book is *by no means* an exhaustive list. It's meant to give you some concrete possibilities, but also to drive a new path to your brain, and let you think about more than just applying to work at someone else's company and working for them. There are *lots* of other possibilities out there. Check them all.

One interesting resource is eHow.com, which has a remarkably large (if not very detailed) list of small businesses that are out there, along with short descriptions of some of the starting steps. The site itself is both interesting and enjoyable. Check it out.

Your local paper probably also has a "services offered" section in the classified ads, maybe even a "services wanted". Read that and see what people are doing, or need done for them.

The local (and not so local) Yellow Pages can also be helpful. See what kind of businesses are working in other parts of the country. Almost all public libraries have a national set of business phone books, so you might start there. Fair warning: sometimes this works and sometimes it doesn't. Some yellow pages are so heavily structured that you won't find the more interesting niche businesses in the area because they don't fit into the categories the phone book sets up. Basically: don't be discouraged if you don't find what you were looking for- it was just one more thing to try.

There is no "help wanted" sign to tell entrepreneurs where their opportunities are. The important thing is to keep your eyes open. Be vigilant. There are a lot of small business opportunities out there, but most people never see them.

# Lessons Learned

Intelligence is the ability to learn from your own mistakes. Wisdom is the ability to learn from *other people's* mistakes.

## Norm's Story: People's names

Everyone says "I'm terrible with names". That's fine. But knowing the name of your customer, their business, and other relations can *really, actually* add to your income.

Norm was genuinely bad with names. Mildly dyslexic and suffering from ADHD, he was an excellent craftsman but was totally lost when it came to people. This cost him time & effort more than once when he asked his accountant to bill BobCo, when he really meant Sam Incorporated. Norm found a way around that: more care in paperwork. Taking the time to create some fill-in-the-blanks forms, so that all the data was there, and taking the time to fill them out completely every time solved the problem for the most part.

Two years later, he applied his solution for paperwork to his problem with faces, and made up some flashcards for his regular customers. He kept them in his truck, and reviewed them before he walked onto the job site. His income from those customers increased by more than 10% over the next year. Expanding that to all of his customers gave him a net of 20%, and better references to boot.

### Lesson: Names matter to your income.

So what if you're bad with names? A monkey can remember a face/name pair for an hour, and there's a genuine financial incentive in it for you. Get past the name thing.

# Dirk's Story: Make your plan happen

Remember that your plan always has three steps:

1. Do some sort of work
2. Charge the customer more than it cost you to do the work
3. Keep the difference

This is often followed by "pay your rent" and "feed your kids", but that's a different book

When you work for someone else, and the plan you're working on doesn't work then you report the problem upline and let them worry about it. The job didn't get done: tell them and wait for further instructions. So what do they want you to do now? Try again? Try something different? What?

When you own your own business, *your* plan is the only thing that matters, since your plan is designed to make you money. This is one time where being flexible is a Very Bad Thing. Your customers (and thus your business plan) are the home team. Assume that everyone else (including your vendors) are the bad guys. Defend your customers from individuals, businesses, or attitudes that might let them down, even accidentally.

Dirk, a businessman I interviewed for this book, needed a printing job done: getting fliers inserted in a local newspaper. He found a frame shop right down the street that also did printing work. We'll call the owner Pete. The conversation went something like this:

> Dirk: *Hi there Pete, I need some printing done for a newspaper advertising insert. It's going to be* [Dirk explains the task] *and I need it by the paper's deadline, which is 10 days from now.*
>
> Pete: *Sure, I can do that. It'll cost* […]
>
> Dirk: *Thanks. I'll call you in a couple days to check up on how things are going.*

Dirk followed up with Pete every few days, either in person or by phone, just to make sure everything was coming along, and Bob assured him that everything was on schedule. Dirk goes down to the printer on the pickup day, and Pete tells him they're not ready, and won't be for 3 more days.

Bad news. The fliers wouldn't be ready for the paper, so his advertising would have to wait for a week. At least, Dirk thinks, the fliers will be ready by then.

More follow-ups, more promises, and surprise, surprise- the fliers are still not ready 3 days later. Dirk's business is now *weeks* behind on its advertising, business is definitely not as good as it should be, and Pete has cost Dirk hundreds, maybe even thousands, of dollars.

Dirk gets wise: First he cancels the original job. No point in giving money to some clown who's just promising over the phone and not delivering in person. Next he gets a new printer. The conversation with the new printer (call him William) goes more like this:

> Dirk: *Hey there William. I'm looking for a printer to do some regular work for me: somewhere around two jobs a month at first, and more later on. I left my last printer because he just couldn't keep his own deadlines, and I absolutely need someone who'll do what they say they'll do. Can you give me any recommendations in this area?*
>
> William (with a smile): *I can handle that.*
>
> Dirk: *I'm not kidding, I really need you to do what you promise. I'm a small business, and a one-day delay can cost me a printing run, which costs me a week of advertising and maybe thousands of dollars. I gave the last guy two chances, but I'm running out of patience.*
>
> William (more seriously): *OK, let's see what we can do.*

And now Dirk is off to a better start. William knows what the stakes are and what Dirk expects. That's the basis for a good business relationship.

*Lesson: Your plan is vital. Defend it.*

Being firm is *not* the same as being rude or bullying people. It's actually a much better and more comfortable situation for both buyer and seller if the requirements are made clear at the beginning.

# Emily's Story: Schedule "other stuff"

Almost everyone who starts their own business naturally spends almost all of their time doing the *job* parts of the job: Carpenters saw and sand, Massage Therapists give massages, Bakers make cookies, etc. It's important to remember that that's usually only half of the work, though. The other parts are less glamorous, and often less satisfying but often every bit as important:

•   Paperwork

- Billing customers
- Making bank deposits
- Paying vendors
- Paying monthly bills
- Advertising
- Marketing
- Keeping a smile on your face when you talk to customers

Lots of things go into a business, and the job-part is only one of them. You really do need to do them all, and for most first-time business owners, this ends up being a problem.

The solution is to schedule the tasks.

Emily was running a small business out of her home, and had a very full schedule during the day while the kids were at school. Her business was successful and growing, and soon filled up every hour between 10am and 3pm. She was thrilled at first, but then everything started to go wrong: bills from vendors were paid late, invoices to her customers didn't go out, tax paperwork was misfiled, etc. Business took a big dip over the next six months, stabilized, and began to grow again. Then three months later the whole cycle started over: trouble, business suffers, stable growth returns.

Emily realized (before too much business was permanently lost) that she needed to schedule the "other stuff", the "back office work" into her workweek just like she scheduled the work she did for her customers. Setting aside Monday mornings for this purpose worked wonders. She had a few less hours to earn money, but her customers (and her partner) were much happier when all the money flowed in and out smoothly.

*Lesson: "The Other Stuff" is boring but necessary.*

At first, make a hard schedule of 5 hours a week of time where you'll handle *only* the office work, and no job work. This will help make sure it gets done.

When you're getting started, doing all the other stuff yourself will really help you learn what's working and what's not. As your business grows, you can farm this work out. The more of this you don't want to do, the more of it you can hire out: a marketing consultant, an accountant, etc. Whether you spend your time or your money doesn't matter. For your business to succeed, it all needs to get done, and done well.

# Business How-To's

## Get and Use a Credit Card Machine

Credit card machines (often called "swipers") are available from companies called "credit clearinghouses". Your bank manager will almost certainly know a few, and any local business that takes credit cards can get you in touch with theirs.

The way it works is pretty simple:

1.  You sign up with the clearinghouse you choose, giving them a bank account number and other information

2.  They give you a credit-card swiping machine which connects to a phone line, the internet, or both. You keep it at your work.

3.  When a customer buys something, you put the amount into the machine, swipe their card, and get their signature. If you're taking numbers over the phone, you can type the number into the machine manually.

4.  The clearinghouse bills their credit card and drops a percentage of the money they billed into your account.

The amount they return to you will vary, usually between 95% and 98%, depending on your credit rating, what card the customer used, and other stuff. The remaining part is kept by the clearinghouse to pay their expenses, etc.

Getting set up is usually free, although sometimes you need to put a deposit on the swiper.

# Get Bonded

For some kinds of work, your customers may want a bond before they hire you. A bond is given by a "trusted third party", called a Bonding Agent. A bond basically says that if you don't do the work legally and competently, the Bonding Agent will directly pay your customer a specific amount of money (the bond amount) and later collect that from you. It's basically a guarantee that you and your work are going to meet the customer's standards.

Think of it like this: You're a small business that the customer has never heard of, but Bob's Bonds has been doing business in your city for 10 years, has a storefront, a reputation, etc. Your customer trusts Bob more than they trust you, so Bob stands behind your work, offering to pay the customer if you don't do the job right.

So how do you get Bob to do that for you? You give Bob information about yourself, and possibly a small percentage of the bond amount. He satisfies himself that he could collect from you if he had to, and then agrees to offer a "bond" on your work.

How big a bond do you need? That depends. If you're repairing lawn mowers, then the price of a lawn mower is pretty much the most damage you could do, so $1,000 is enough. If you're doing large aquarium maintenance in an unattended home, you could probably do a *lot* of damage, so you might be nearer $20,000.

# Upgrade Your Vehicle Insurance.

In most cases, in most states, your vehicle does *not* require special insurance if you use it for transportation to and from work. This is true even if you transport tools or materials. So for most people, most of the jobs in this book will *not* require you to change your vehicle insurance. As always, check with your insurer first.

If your vehicle *is* your business, such as a snowplow or well drilling rig, then that's different. For work like that, you will almost certainly need Commercial Vehicle Insurance. You will also (probably) need to register (or re-register) the vehicle as a commercial vehicle with your state Department of Motor Vehicles. Commercial Vehicle Insurance is available from most major insurers, although not always from the discount brands that advertise on TV.

In this area *in particular* you should shop around. A lot. It's not uncommon to have the same insurance cost 30% more / less from different insurers. That could be thousands of dollars per year.

# Conclusion

## - - - ACCESS GRANTED - - -

There are many ways to earn a living, and being employed by someone else is the only one most people ever consider. Hopefully this book has shown you that there are alternatives, and given you some encouragement to move beyond being an "employee".

You now have access to thirty five new ways to make money, none of which require an interview, and any of which you could begin building today. Dozens of others await your discovery.

Having your own business offers both freedom and control. In exchange for the broader responsibilities you accept, you have better pay, greater job security, and more control over your time. The choices are all yours.

# APPENDIX A: SUMMARY OF JOBS

| Job | Pay | Training | Equipment | Licensing |
|---|---|---|---|---|
| Animal Caretaker | $ | Informal | $ | None |
| Animal Control Technician | $$ | Informal | $$ | City/State |
| Bicycle Courier | $$ | Informal | $ | None |
| Carpenter | $$+ | Formal | $$ | State |
| Crime Scene Cleanup | $$ | Formal | $$ | City/State |
| Dance Instructor | $$ | Informal | $ | None |
| Dog Walker | $ | Informal | $ | None |
| Electrician | $$$ | Formal | $$+ | State |
| Exterminator | $$ | Formal | $$ | City/State |
| Farrier | $$ | Informal | $$ | See Job |
| Gold Panner | Open | None | $ | None |
| Handyman | $ | None | $ | None |
| Language Teacher | $+ | Informal | $ | None |
| Large Aquarium Maintenance | $+ | None | $+ | None |
| Limousine Driver | $+ | Informal | $$ | None* |
| Locksmith | $$ | Formal | $+ | Many States |
| Marine Logger | Open | | $$$ | SCUBA |
| Meteor Hunter | Open | None | $+ | None |
| Mobile Car Detailing | $$ | None | $$ | None |
| Music Teacher | $$ | Informal | $ | None |
| Obedience Trainer | $ | None | $+ | None |
| Painter | $$ | Informal | $$ | State |

| Job | Pay | Training | Equipment | Licensing |
|---|---|---|---|---|
| Personal Fitness Trainer | $+ | Informal | $$ | None |
| Plumber | $$$ | Formal | $$$ | State |
| Pool & Spa Maintenance | $$ | Informal | $$ | None |
| Rental Property Manager | $$ | Informal | $ | None |
| Sign Language Interpreter | $$ | Formal | $ | National |
| Snow Plow Operator | $+ | Informal | $$+ | None |
| Taxidermist | $ | Informal | $ | State / National |
| Tile & Ceramics Contractor | $$$ | Formal | $$ | State |
| Tow Truck Operator | $$ | Informal | $$+ | None |
| Traveling Massage Therapist | $$ | Informal or Formal | $$ | State |
| Traveling Pet Groomer | $+ | Informal | $+ | None |
| Well Driller | $$$ | Informal | $$$ | Many States |
| Worm Fiddler | Open | None | $ | None |

The foraging professions' pay is listed as "open" because it's really defined as "All you can gather and sell." Worms may be limited on the sale side, and gold may be limited on the gathering side, but the sky is the limit.

The licensing data here is gathered and offered informally. It is obviously subject to changes in city, state, and national law. You should always check with the local authorities and/or people who are already in that business for the "local ground-truth".

# Appendix B: Add-on businesses

## The Dangers of Mini- or Side- businesses

Everyone's been to the local shop that started out as a mailbox store, but now sells candy, books, inspirational plaques, greeting cards, wall hangings, phone cards, magazines, stamps, and all natural life-enhancing specialty fruit juice products. It's not a pretty thing.

There are lots of "mini" jobs available, but the trick is to avoid the ones that will take more time, effort, or reputation than they return. In general, it's safe to decide against anything that isn't your core business. If you do add an on-the-side income stream, revisit it every year to see if it's earning it's keep.

Here are a few examples of mini-businesses that might complement your existing business.

## Notary Public

A notary public is someone who administers oaths, takes affidavits, and witnesses and authenticates the execution of certain classes of documents. Their powers vary from state to state. Having things like loan documents, or contracts, "notarized" is a simple and relatively inexpensive way to establish a legal paper trail.

If you're in the legal, municipal, or contracting spaces, you may be in a position to offer notary services from time to time, and pick up some extra income in this way.

In California, becoming a notary public is just a matter of attending a few hours of class and passing an exam. In other states the process can be more complicated, or less.

## Key Duplication

Key duplication is available in a lot of facilities, including many mall "stand businesses", home improvement stores, and, obviously, from professional locksmiths. The money to be made is small (often a dollar or so per key) but it's money nonetheless, and there's demand for it.

Getting a key duplicating machine is fairly simple. You will also (in most states) be required to register as a key duplicator, but there's usually no test or anything.

## Stuff for Sale

Beware the ever-expanding "stuff I sell" monster. It can soak up your time while making your overall business look less professional.

Having said that, if you're a pet groomer, having the odd bow, collar, leash, or carrier visibly for sale is often worth the trouble. Likewise if you're a tile repair specialist and you consistently talk up a particular tile cleaner, having some for sale (rather than just referring people to a Web site) is a good idea and will please the customer.

Every business transaction that brings you into direct contact with a happy customer is also a bit of an opportunity to expand what you do for them, and earn a bit of extra money in the process.

*Never* feel obligated to traffic in salable items, though- if you don't want to, by all means don't.

# Appendix C: Other Resources

## Small Business Development Centers

SBDCs provide educational services for prospective small business owners. They are local partnerships between the government, colleges and universities, and are are administered by the U.S. Small Business Administration. See http://www.sba.gov/sbdc

## Your Chamber of Commerce

The value of these varies dramatically from place to place. In some places it's a kind of statussy club, where everyone's trying to impress everyone else. In other cases, it's a gold mine of references, pointers, free help, encouragement, and advice. You don't have to belong, and if you do belong, you don't have to belong to *just* one: you can usually be a member of the chamber of all the local towns. Shop around, you'll find the right one.

## The Better Business Bureau (BBB)

The Better Business Bureau is a great resource for small businesses. Too many small business owners regard the BBB as "the enemy", storing up all the complaints that have been lodged against them. Complaints *will* happen. Don't sweat it. The BBB has classes and materials for small business owners to help with all sorts of small business problems. They make a much better asset than enemy. Use them.

## Other local small-business resources

In larger cities there are often Small Business Councils and similar organizations, kind of like a Chamber of Commerce for people smaller than Sears and Wal-Mart. Keep an eye out. There are a lot of other people in your position as a small business, and there's wisdom in many minds.